P9-CJR-194

JOHN BROWN'S RAID ON HARPERS FERRY IN AMERICAN HISTORY

Other titles *in American History*

IN
AMERICAN
HISTORY

JOHN BROWN'S RAID ON HARPERS FERRY IN AMERICAN HISTORY

R. Conrad Stein

Enslow Publishers, Inc.

40 Industrial Road	PO Box 38
Box 398	Aldershot
Berkeley Heights, NJ 07922	Hants GU12 6BP
USA	UK

http://www.enslow.com

TETON COUNTY LIBRARY
JACKSON, WYOMING

Copyright © 1999 by R. Conrad Stein

All rights reserved.

No part of this book may be reproduced by any means
without the written permission of the publisher.

Library of Congress Cataloging-in-Publication Data

Stein, R. Conrad.
    John Brown's raid on Harpers Ferry in American history / R. Conrad
Stein.
        p. cm. — (In American history)
    Includes bibliographical references and index.
    Summary: Explores the people and events connected with John
Brown's attempted slave uprising in Harpers Ferry in 1859.
    ISBN 0-7660-1123-2
    1. Harpers Ferry (W. Va.)—History—John Brown's Raid, 1859—
Juvenile literature. 2. Brown, John, 1800–1859—Juvenile literature.
[1. Harpers Ferry (W. Va.)—History—John Brown's Raid, 1859.
2. Brown, John, 1800–1859. 3. Abolitionists.] I. Title. II. Series.
E451.S85 1999
973.7'116—dc21   98-35950
                                           CIP
                                          AC

Printed in the United States of America

10 9 8 7 6 5 4 3 2 1

To Our Readers:
All Internet addresses in this book were active and appropriate when we
went to press. Any comments or suggestions can be sent by e-mail to
Comments@enslow.com or to the address on the back cover.

Illustration Credits: Enslow Publishers, Inc., p. 24; Library of
Congress, pp. 8, 19, 33, 34, 40, 49, 51, 61, 83, 84, 89, 93, 98, 105,
111; R. Conrad Stein, p. 9; National Archives, pp. 13, 15, 26, 28, 44,
78, 81, 108, 112, 113; Photo courtesy of Harpers Ferry National
Historical Park, pp. 63, 68, 74.

Cover Illustration: National Archives; Photo Courtesy of Harpers
Ferry National Historical Park.

★ CONTENTS ★

*J*ohn Brown of Osawatomie

Spake on his dying day,

I will not have, to shrive my soul

A priest in Slavery's pay;

But let some poor slave-mother

Whom I have striven to free

With her children, from the gallows-stair,

Put up a prayer for me!

—Poet John Greenleaf Whittier (1807–1892), reflecting on the execution of John Brown in his poem "Brown of Osawatomie"[1]

1

EXECUTION AT CHARLES TOWN

Scene at the Courthouse

Some fifteen hundred soldiers lined the streets of Charles Town, Virginia (now West Virginia), on December 2, 1859. Tension gripped the normally quiet community. The most talked-about American of the moment, John Brown, was about to meet his death on the gallows. Weeks earlier, Brown and twenty-one followers had seized an armory in the nearby town of Harpers Ferry. Brown wanted to give the rifles in the armory to slaves and lead them in a mass rebellion against their masters. He envisioned the start of a massive race war, a war that would rid the United States of its greatest sin—slavery.

The courthouse in Charles Town, Virginia (today West Virginia), as it looked during John Brown's time.

The raid at Harpers Ferry failed miserably. More than a dozen men were killed, and Brown was taken prisoner. He was sentenced to hang for leading the raid. His impending death had all of Virginia rife with rumors. Some rumors said armies of antislavery fanatics were poised in the woods outside of town, ready to rescue their hero. A few Americans believed that the hand of God would miraculously snatch the condemned man from his jail cell and carry him to heaven.

Finally, the door to the Jefferson County Courthouse opened. White-haired and bearded, the fifty-nine-year-old John Brown stepped out, flanked

A historical marker in Jefferson County, West Virginia, reminds people that the most famous trial of the pre-Civil War period took place here.

by guards. For weeks, his name and drawings of his face had appeared on the front pages of just about every newspaper in the United States. He was the subject of passionate arguments held in coffeehouses, at general stores, and wherever else Americans gathered. Some people spat out his name. John Brown was a murderer, cried angry men and women. He was a savior, claimed others. He was a martyr. He was a madman. He was a saint.

On this day of execution, however, witnesses agreed that John Brown looked calm, even serene. His arms were tied behind his back at the elbows in what must have been a painful position. Yet his eyes gazed straight ahead at the sun-drenched streets and ranks of soldiers. His face showed no sign of discomfort or fear. A horse-drawn wagon bearing a coffin—his coffin— stood waiting. John Brown and his guards moved toward the wagon. Straining against the ropes that bound his arms, the bearded man gave one of his guards a note. The first line of the note read, "I John Brown am now quite *certain* that the crimes of this *guilty, land: will* never be purged *away* but with Blood."[2]

A HOUSE DIVIDED

A house divided against itself cannot stand." I believe this government cannot endure permanently half slave and half free.

—Abraham Lincoln, candidate for the United States Senate from Illinois, speaking in 1858[1]

Slavery, the Peculiar Institution

"All men are created equal," read the stirring words of the Declaration of Independence of the United States. Yet at the time those words were written, slavery was legal in all of the thirteen colonies. Soon after American independence, slavery began to fade out in the Northern states. However, the slave system remained in full force in the South. In 1859, the year of John Brown's execution, the population of the United States totaled 31 million people. Of those, roughly one in every eight was a slave.

"No day ever dawns for the slave, nor is it looked for," said one freed black man. "For the slave it is night—all night, forever."[2] Slaves lived in conditions so miserable it is difficult to imagine their circumstances today. On Southern farms ten to fifteen slaves were packed together in dirt-floor cabins no bigger than a modern one-car garage. There was no furniture in the slave quarters. Beds were made of straw and old rags. Killer diseases such as cholera, yellow fever, malaria, and tuberculosis swept through the crowded slave communities, taking countless lives. Because of poor diet and inadequate medical care, slave children were infested with worms and had rotten teeth. Fewer than four out of every one hundred slaves lived to be sixty years of age.

Work for a slave field hand began at dawn and lasted until sundown. If a full moon illuminated the fields, the work went on far into the evening. House slaves, who performed duties as servants and cooks in the master's quarters, had a lighter workload than the field hand. Some slaves were skilled carpenters, blacksmiths, bricklayers, and barrel makers. One of the most dreaded jobs in slave society was coal mining. Slaves compelled to work in the dark, damp coal shafts almost always died young.

The master had complete power over the lives of his slaves. This meant the master was free to choose what sort of punishment should be dealt to a disobedient slave or one whose work did not meet his standards. Some owners punished slaves by withholding food or by threatening to sell a cherished son or daughter. Many owners relied on the whip. A slave named Solomon Northrop remembered being tied to a tree and savagely beaten: "I prayed for mercy, but my prayer was only answered with imprecations [curses] and with stripes. I thought I must die beneath the

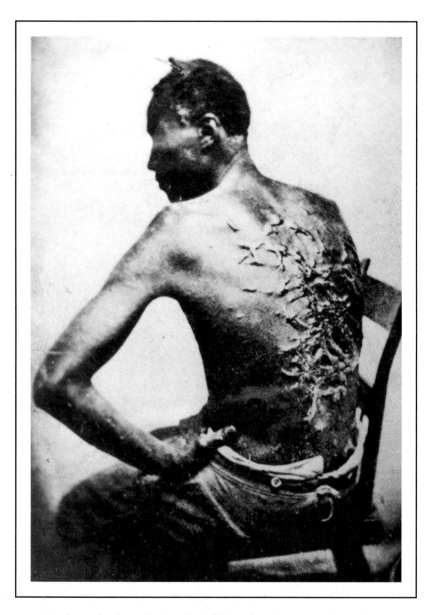

A slave displays the results of his whipping in a photo taken in Baton Rouge, Louisiana, on April 2, 1863.

lashes. . . . My sufferings I can compare to nothing else than the burning agonies of hell!"[3]

As bad as everyday life was for a slave, he or she lived in terror of being sold. Sale to a farm in a faraway community meant leaving brothers, sisters, and other loved ones. Yet a slave could expect to be sold at least once in his or her lifetime. If sold at public auction, the slave was forced to stand, often naked, in front of perspective buyers. Interested buyers examined the slave's teeth and limbs as they would inspect an animal in a pen. Slaves at auction were told to jump and to lift objects to prove their strength and dexterity. "Them days was hell," remembered a slave woman. "Babies was snatched from their mother's breast and sold. . . . Children was separated from sisters and brothers and never saw each other again. Course they cried. You think they not cry when they was sold like cattle?"[4]

In the North people generally disagreed with slavery, but they were reluctant to interfere with the practices prevalent in the South. Slavery was not as necessary or as profitable in the North. Northern businessmen relied on European immigrants as a source of cheap labor. Many Northern leaders overlooked the evils of slavery because cotton, picked by slaves, was the nation's most profitable export. Cotton required the work of many field hands. One New York City cotton merchant wrote,

> There are millions upon millions of dollars due from
> Southerners to the merchants and mechanics of this
> city alone, the payment of which would be jeopardized

by any rupture between the North and South. We cannot afford to let [antislavery people] overthrow slavery. It is not a matter of principle with us. It is a matter of business necessity.[5]

Few people asked the slaves what they thought of a custom and set of laws that viewed them as property, without any rights. Slaves were the victims of what was politely called the South's "peculiar institution."

The slaves survived and fought the system in many subtle and ingenious ways. To rebuke an unkind

A pen in a slave market, where slaves were locked up before they were sold.

master, all slaves on a farm or a plantation might join in a secret work slowdown. During such a slowdown, farming instruments would mysteriously break or get lost, thus endangering the harvest. Slaves also found strength in religion, which developed as a blend of African and Christian beliefs. Music provided relief from the constant grind of toil and fear. And the hope for freedom on some distant day lingered in their dreams. Slaves who were skilled workers might be able to get paid for extra jobs, save their pennies, and buy their freedom. Some slaves were given their freedom by generous masters. For most field hands, however, the only hope of finding freedom was to run away.

Attempting escape took courage and daring. In Southern states slaves were not allowed to walk on roads alone without the written permission of their masters. If an escapee were caught and returned to the master, the slave could be branded with a hot iron or whipped almost to the point of death. Still, slaves slipped away in bold attempts to find freedom. Some historians estimate that as many as one hundred thousand slaves fled from their masters between 1830 and 1860. Escaped slaves sought refuge in black communities in Northern states, or they journeyed to Canada, where slavery did not exist.

White Southerners dreaded the ultimate form of slave resistance: mass insurrection. In several Southern states slaves outnumbered whites. What if all the slaves in a community suddenly picked up clubs or knives and attacked their owners? Such an onslaught

SOURCE DOCUMENT

I KEPT A DEPOT ON WHAT WAS CALLED THE UNDERGROUND RAILWAY. IT WAS CALLED [UNDERGROUND] BECAUSE THOSE WHO TOOK PASSAGE ON IT DISAPPEARED FROM PUBLIC VIEW AS IF THEY HAD GONE INTO THE GROUND. AFTER THE FUGITIVE SLAVES ENTERED A DEPOT ON THAT ROAD, NO TRACE OF THEM COULD BE FOUND. THEY WERE SECRETLY PASSED FROM ONE DEPOT TO ANOTHER UNTIL THEY ARRIVED IN CANADA. THIS ROAD EXTENDED THROUGH ALL THE FREE STATES. . . . THERE WAS NO SECRET SOCIETY ORGANIZED. THERE WERE NO SECRET OATHS TAKEN. . . . AND YET THERE WERE NO BETRAYALS. ANTISLAVERY PERSONS WERE ACTUATED BY A SENSE OF HUMANITY AND RIGHT, AND OF COURSE WERE TRUE TO ONE ANOTHER.[6]

Many hundreds of slaves escaped with the help of the Underground Railroad, an organization of blacks and whites that assisted runaways on their journey north. The organization used railroad terms in its work. For example, houses where escapees could rest were called "depots," guides were called "conductors," and the escapees were "passengers." One "stationmaster" on the Underground Railroad was the Reverend John Rankin of Ohio, who explained his experience.

by people made furious after generations of bondage would result in a horrible bloodbath. In 1831 a slave preacher named Nat Turner led such a rebellion in Virginia. Some sixty whites, many of them women and children, were killed by Turner and his followers. The Virginia militia suppressed the rebellion, and the state hanged twenty slaves, including Nat Turner. Fearful whites also killed at least one hundred innocent slaves whom they suspected of being Turner sympathizers. Several other slave uprisings had rocked the South before the time of Nat Turner. It is no wonder that John Brown's attempt to organize a large-scale slave revolt caused such panic in the slave-owning society.

Only about three hundred fifty thousand Southern whites—one family out of four—owned slaves. Yet even whites who did not own slaves argued that no one should tamper with the age-old laws that permitted slavery in Southern states. Slavery was held as a "state's right." Any attempt by the federal government to emancipate (free) the slaves was looked upon as a violation of states' rights and an insult to Southern honor.

To justify their peculiar institution, some Southerners painted an ideal picture of slave society. Preachers claimed that slavery "civilized" black people by introducing them to Christianity. Southern ladies and gentlemen pointed out that they treated their slaves as members of their own family—and in some cases this was true. But not all could close their eyes to the vile side of slavery. One white woman who had recently moved from the North to a sugar plantation in Louisiana wrote in her diary, "Oh, how my ears have been stunned today by the cry of the distressed. How bestial it is to whip the Negro so; surely God will not wink at such cruelty."[7]

The House Divides

In the first half of the nineteenth century, heated arguments over slavery began to separate the United States into two camps—North and South, antislavery and proslavery—each camp hostile to the other. Year by year through the first half of the 1800s, the passions grew. Thomas Jefferson, the nation's third president

The idealistic Southern view of slave life depicted healthy, carefree slaves enjoying life despite their circumstances.

and himself a slave owner, said the issue of slavery alarmed the land and frightened the people like "a fire bell [ringing] in the night."[8]

By the 1850s, the most contentious issue dividing the country concerned the new states opening up in the West. The South wanted frontier territories to develop as slave states, whereas the North envisioned them as free states. This issue first surfaced in 1820 when an agreement called the Missouri Compromise allowed Missouri to enter the Union as a slave state, but only if Maine joined as a free state. It also established a boundary at 36°30' latitude, above which slavery would not be permitted. A similar agreement, the Compromise of 1850, permitted California to come in as a free state, whereas the question of slavery in Utah and New Mexico was left open for residents to decide in the future.

The compromises did little to soothe tempers stirring in the nation. In fact, most government measures only added fuel to an already raging fire. As part of the Compromise of 1850, Congress made a concession to the South by passing the Fugitive Slave Law. The law allowed owners and their agents to pursue runaway slaves into the Northern states. Antislavery Northerners literally waged war against the act, hiding runaway slaves in their homes and, if necessary, defending them with guns.

The Southern proslavery cause was bolstered in 1857 by a famous Supreme Court case called the *Dred Scott* decision. In the case, the Supreme Court held that slaves were "property" and, therefore, had no rights under the nation's Constitution. The *Dred Scott* decision strengthened the legal authority of the slave states. But the case infuriated opponents of slavery and further inflamed the national temper.

The slavery question turned Washington, D.C., into a battleground. Fistfights and worse broke out among the nation's leaders. Senators and representatives carried guns and knives with them to congressional meetings because tempers had worn so thin and arguments had grown so fiery. In 1856 Charles Sumner, a senator from Massachusetts, made a speech denouncing slavery. The very next day Preston Brooks, a congressman from South Carolina, marched up to Sumner in the Senate chamber and beat him over the head with a thick cane. Brooks hit Sumner so many times and so violently that the cane broke. Sumner spent years recovering from his injuries. Brooks's grateful South Carolina neighbors sent him new canes to replace the one he had shattered on Sumner's head.

In 1854 Congress passed the Kansas-Nebraska Act, another attempt to deal with the slavery question in developing states. The terms of the Kansas-Nebraska Act established two new territories, Kansas and Nebraska, and allowed them to become either slave states or free, depending on the will of their voters. This idea was called popular sovereignty. Foes of slavery condemned the Kansas-Nebraska Act because it permitted slavery to become established in a region

SOURCE DOCUMENT

THE [FRAMERS OF THE CONSTITUTION] PERFECTLY UNDERSTOOD THE MEANING OF THE LANGUAGE THEY USED AND HOW IT WOULD BE UNDERSTOOD BY OTHERS; AND THEY KNEW THAT IT WOULD NOT IN ANY PART OF THE CIVILIZED WORLD BE SUPPOSED TO EMBRACE THE NEGRO RACE, WHICH, BY COMMON CONSENT, HAD BEEN EXCLUDED FROM CIVILIZED GOVERNMENTS AND THE FAMILY OF NATIONS AND DOOMED TO SLAVERY. . . . THE UNHAPPY BLACK RACE WERE SEPARATED FROM THE WHITE. . . . AND WERE NEVER THOUGHT OF OR SPOKEN OF EXCEPT AS PROPERTY AND WHEN THE CLAIMS OF THE OWNER OR THE PROFIT OF THE TRADER WERE SUPPOSED TO NEED PROTECTION.[9]

In the 1830s, the slave Dred Scott traveled with his master to Illinois, the Wisconsin Territory, and the Louisiana Territory, regions where slavery was forbidden. After his master's death, Scott sued for his freedom, saying that his bonds of slavery should have ended when he stepped on free soil. In the Dred Scott decision, Supreme Court Chief Justice Roger Taney, whose family owned slaves, wrote that no black person—free or slave—was a citizen of the United States. Therefore, no black person deserved protection under the Constitution.

where it had previously been banned by the Missouri Compromise. Thousands of antislavery Americans, including John Brown and his family, rushed to Kansas and Nebraska to swell the vote count and to add their voices to the cause.

The compromises and government action of the 1850s satisfied few Americans and angered most. In fact, many historians view the compromises of the 1850s as stepping-stones toward civil war.

No amount of Washington agreements could halt the wave of hatred swelling in both the North and the South. Certainly the North did not speak with one voice on the slavery issue. A large percentage of Northerners, including those who opposed slavery, wanted to make no bold moves to end the practice because they feared it would start a war between Northern and Southern states.

The Abolitionists

In the North a new breed of antislavery crusaders stepped forth between 1830 and 1860, demanding immediate emancipation even at the price of war. Under their direction, the antislavery cause became a crusade led by firebrand speakers and preachers called abolitionists.

The abolitionists insisted that the nation end slavery, *abolishing* the institution at once and forever. They would accept no compromise and hear no debate. Their position on slavery—though radical at the time—is similar to how most people today feel about

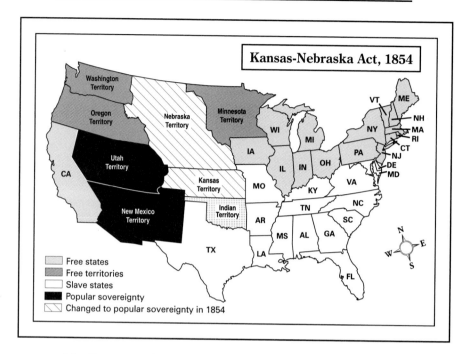

The Kansas-Nebraska Act of 1854 allowed the residents of the newly created Kansas and Nebraska territories to decide for themselves whether to allow slavery within their borders. This map shows how the states and territories were affected by the act.

the matter: The notion that one person can own another person is socially, morally, politically, and religiously wrong.

Frederick Douglass was one of the great abolitionists of the era. Born a slave, Douglass ran away from his master at age nineteen. After he found freedom he wrote books, spoke out against slavery, and published an abolitionist newspaper called the *North Star*. In a letter to his former master, Douglass said,

What you are, I am. You are a man and so am I. God
created both, and made us separate beings. I am not
by nature bond to you, or you to me. I cannot walk
upon your legs . . . I cannot breathe for you. . . . In
leaving you, I took nothing but what belonged to me.[10]

The letter captured the essence of the abolitionist
argument, that slavery violated natural law, and no
human-made law could possibly legitimize the practice.

William Lloyd Garrison was an especially ardent
abolitionist. He was jailed several times for his out-
spoken views, and his life was threatened by proslavery
men. Despite the dangers he faced, Garrison published
a newspaper, *The Liberator*, which demanded an immediate end to slavery. In editorials his newspaper said
slavery must be destroyed even if its destruction led to
a bloody war between the states. Garrison once held a
copy of the United States Constitution before a crowd
and burned it because the document had allowed
slavery to continue.

Abolitionists were denounced as troublemakers in
many Northern communities, and they were hated in
the South. After passage of the Fugitive Slave Law,
those who helped slaves escape to freedom were law-
breakers who could be jailed or even hanged for their
offenses. Yet in the 1850s—as the national mood
became more and more stormy—the abolition movement grew in strength and in numbers.

Some of the most courageous abolitionists were
women. Many historians have pointed out that women
were perhaps more sympathetic toward slaves than

Born into slavery in Maryland, Frederick Douglass (1817–1895) escaped when he was nineteen. He then became one of the nation's most famous abolitionists, tirelessly speaking and writing for the cause of emancipation.

were men because women also had few legal rights in nineteenth-century America. By law, women could not vote, and in many states they could not inherit property. Harriet Beecher Stowe created a powerful abolitionist testament with her novel *Uncle Tom's Cabin*. A moment of high drama in the story came when a slave woman fled from bondage by crossing the icy Ohio River with her baby in her arms. *Uncle Tom's Cabin* so infuriated slave owners that in some Southern states just having a copy in one's home could mean a jail sentence for the home owner. At the time, a less famous abolitionist, one who had to keep her views secret, was ex-slave Harriet Tubman. In 1849, Tubman escaped from her master after he struck her on the head with an iron bar. She returned to the South time and time again as a conductor on the Underground Railroad and led more than three hundred slaves north to freedom. Harriet Tubman was compared with the great freedom-giver of the Bible and is remembered as "the Moses of her people."

Another early abolitionist was Elijah Parish Lovejoy. In 1837 Lovejoy began printing an abolitionist newspaper in the southern Illinois town of Alton. At least three times mobs broke into Lovejoy's office and smashed his printing press. One night Lovejoy saw a group of men approach the warehouse where his new press was stored. He dashed into the street to defend his property. A shot rang out. Lovejoy lay in the dust, bleeding to death.

Harriet Beecher Stowe (1811–1896) first published Uncle
Tom's Cabin *in 1852. The book exposed the cruelties of
slave life and aroused both Northerners and Southerners
to action.*

Across the country abolitionist preachers and poets cried out against the murder of Elijah Lovejoy. In the Congregational Church in Hudson, Ohio, a preacher named Laurens P. Hickok said, "The crisis has come. The question now before American citizens is no longer, 'Can the slaves be made free?' but are we free or are we slaves under Southern mob law?"[11] Hickok then allowed church members to stand up and state their views. A thin man in his late thirties raised his hand to be recognized. The man stood. According to his daughter, who sat beside him, the man said, "Here before God, in the presence of these witnesses from this time, I consecrate my life to the destruction of slavery."[12]

He was John Brown, perhaps the most forceful abolitionist of them all.

Blow ye the trumpet, blow.

Sweet is Thy work, my God, my King.

I'll praise my Maker with my breath.

O', happy is the man who hears.

Why should we start, and fear to die.

With songs and honors sounding loud.

Ah, lovely appearance of death.

THE MAKING OF A MARTYR

—From Isaac Watts's song "Blow Ye the Trumpet, Blow," John Brown's favorite hymn[1]

A Calvinistic Faith

Calvinism—more a philosophy than an organized religion—was practiced by many Americans early in the nation's history. It was named after one of the leaders of the Protestant Reformation, John Calvin, who lived in the 1500s. Those who subscribed to Calvinism believed that men and women were born wicked and that only a chosen few could expect to be spared the doom of hell. It was a stern belief, one that demanded long hours of prayer and a life of sacrifice. Owen Brown, the father of John Brown, was a Calvinist. All of Owen Brown's children were brought up under strict Calvinistic codes.

SOURCE DOCUMENT

THE WRATH OF GOD BURNS AGAINST [SINNERS]; THEIR DAMNATION DOES NOT SLUMBER; THE PIT IS PREPARED; THE FIRE IS MADE READY TO RECEIVE THEM; THE FLAMES DO NOW RAGE AND GLOW. THE GLITTERING SWORD IS WHET AND HELD OVER THEM, AND THE PIT HAS OPENED HER MOUTH UNDER THEM. . . . SO THAT THUS IT IS THAT NATURAL MEN ARE HELD IN THE HAND OF GOD OVER THE PIT OF HELL; THEY HAVE DESERVED THE FIERY PIT AND ARE ALREADY SENTENCED TO IT. . . . THE DEVIL IS WAITING FOR THEM; HELL IS GAPING FOR THEM; THE FLAMES GATHER AND FLASH ABOUT THEM. . . . IN SHORT [SINNERS] HAVE NO REFUGE, NOTHING TO TAKE HOLD OF. . . .[2]

The most influential of American Calvinists was Jonathan Edwards (1703–1758), a pastor who practiced in Connecticut and Massachusetts. John Brown read many of Edwards's sermons, including his most famous one, "Sinners in the Hands of an Angry God." Typical of Calvinistic doctrine, the sermon describes a vengeful God, a terrible vision of hell, and a condemnation of men and women who are imprisoned by their own sins.

John Brown was born on May 9, 1800, in Torrington, Connecticut, the third of six children. He grew up in a poor but respected family in the community. The Browns could trace their family roots back to the Pilgrims who sailed on the *Mayflower* and landed at what is now Plymouth, Massachusetts, in 1620.

When John Brown was five years old, his father moved the family to the Ohio village of Hudson. At the time, Ohio was frontier country. One of John's best childhood friends was a Seneca Indian boy who lived in a nearby camp. John spent so much time in the camp that he learned some of the Seneca language. One day his friend gave John a yellow marble. He cherished the marble but carelessly lost it in the woods. John cried so hard over the marble that only his mother could console him. As a child John Brown regularly took his hurts to his mother rather than to his stern father.

When John was eight, his baby sister died. Her sudden death made his mother sick with grief. She would not eat and grew pale and thin. She died on December 9, 1808. John's father remarried, and John adjusted to life with his stepmother. But in a letter John claimed, "[I] continued to pine after [my] own mother for years."[3]

John's father taught him religion

Owen Brown, John Brown's father, raised his children to follow the strict doctrines of Calvinism.

John Brown was born in this house in Torrington, Connecticut, in May 1800.

with stern Calvinistic principles. He also lectured John on the evils of slavery. Abolitionism was neither a strong movement in America in the early 1800s nor was it a Calvinistic issue. Yet Owen Brown was a firm abolitionist who regularly and loudly denounced slavery as a terrible sin.

Life on the Ohio frontier emphasized hard work and fervent religious beliefs for the Brown family. Church and toil consumed John's boyhood. John studied basic reading and writing in a log schoolhouse in Hudson. From his father, he learned the tanning trade—how to make leather from animal hides. Tanning would provide his livelihood in later life.

At about age twelve, John participated in a cattle drive that brought him to Kentucky and required him to stay several nights in the house of a United States marshal. At first, young John thought the marshal was a fine gentleman. The marshal owned a slave boy about John's age. John felt sorry for the boy because he looked ill-clothed and poorly fed. Moreover, the young slave seemed lonely and confused, as he had recently been separated from his mother and father. One day, the boy made some trifling mistake. The marshal picked up an iron shovel and gave the slave boy a terrible beating right before John's eyes. John was too young to say or do anything to stop the beating, but he never forgot the shocking sight. He later wrote that the experience "made [me] a most *determined Abolitionist* [the emphasis is Brown's] and led [me] to declare or *Swear: Eternal war* with slavery."[4]

In his teenage years, John worked in a tannery owned by his father. At night he studied the Bible, searching for God's will. He found in the Scriptures rules for living that he believed were heaven-sent. He had no tolerance for those who, in his opinion, violated biblical laws. John sometimes made his own friends uncomfortable with the deadly serious tone that overtook him when he discussed the Bible and spoke of the horrible punishments God had in store for those who ignored the book's tenets.

In his readings, John determined that the Bible condemned slavery as a moral evil. Ironically, during that era thousands of other Americans quoted biblical

SOURCE DOCUMENT

JOHN WAS NEVER QUARRELSOME; BUT WAS EXCESSIVELY FOND OF THE HARDEST AND ROUGHEST KIND OF PLAYS. . . . INDEED WHEN FOR A SHORT TIME HE WAS SENT TO SCHOOL THE OPPORTUNITY IT AFFORDED TO WRESTLE AND SNOWBALL AND RUN AND JUMP AND KNOCK OFF OLD SEEDY WOOL HATS OFFERED TO HIM ALMOST THE ONLY COMPENSATION FOR THE CONFINEMENT AND RESTRAINTS OF SCHOOL. . . . TO BE SENT OFF THROUGH THE WILDERNESS TO VERY CONSIDERABLE DISTANCES WAS PARTICULARLY HIS DELIGHT . . . BY THE TIME HE WAS TWELVE-YEARS-OLD HE WAS SENT OFF MORE THAN A HUNDRED MILES WITH COMPANIES OF CATTLE; & HE WOULD HAVE THOUGHT HIS CHARACTER MUCH INJURED HAD HE OBLIGED TO BE HELPED IN ANY SUCH JOB.[5]

In 1857, John Brown answered a request from one of his supporters and wrote a letter to twelve-year-old Henry Stearns of Boston, telling of his own childhood in Ohio. John Brown described the letter as a "short Story," and therefore wrote in the third person, referring to the boy John Brown as "John" or "he" rather than "I."

passages that they claimed justified the practice of slavery. Many Southern preachers cried out from their pulpits that God demanded that masters keep slaves.

To Brown, the religious arguments for slavery were themselves blasphemy. To hold the Bible in one hand and a whip in another was a double sin, against both God and the enslaved. Brown came to believe that slavery was a national sin, one that stained the souls of all Americans. Not until slavery was abolished could any American—from the North or the South—expect to be saved from hell.

Even as a youth, Brown was not content merely to speak out against slavery. Before he reached the age of twenty, he had already helped one slave escape to freedom in Canada. And he made it clear to anyone who would listen that he would aid all runaway slaves. If runaways needed help, all they had to do was knock on John Brown's door.

The Middle Years—Tragedy and Frustration

When he was twenty, Brown married Dianthe Lusk of Hudson, Ohio. She was a religious young woman and a hardworking homemaker. Children came quickly. Three sons were born before Brown turned twenty-four. In 1825, Brown moved his family to Randolph, Pennsylvania, where he bought a farm and started a tannery business. It was the first of many such moves, and it began a series of frustrating business failures. Over the next thirty years, John Brown opened and closed fifteen different businesses in four different states. For most of his life, he was in debt to bankers and to various business partners.

Worst of all, death haunted the Brown household. In frontier America there were no vaccinations to protect people from killer diseases. Medical care was primitive or nonexistent. Death came to children so frequently that many farm parents claimed they did not want to become attached to their little ones until they reached the age of about six and had a better chance of surviving. In 1831, Brown's four-year-old son died. The next year, his wife became sick and died also. In twelve years she had given birth to seven children, two of whom died young. Brown mourned the losses. Years later he said that after his wife's death, "[I] had a steady, strong desire to die."[6]

Brown remarried within a year, this time to Mary Day, who was only sixteen. In all, Brown would father twenty children with his two wives. Of the twenty, nine died in infancy or early childhood. In a terrible kitchen accident, a one-year-old daughter was scalded to death. During the autumn of 1843, an epidemic of dysentery swept the community and four of Brown's children died within a few months. Brown buried them in a row and planted crosses to mark the graves. Even on the frontier, where death came suddenly and cruelly, the Brown family suffered death's agony to a greater degree than did their neighbors.

The passing of beloved children, however, could not shatter Brown's Calvinistic faith. To him, the family's bitter misfortunes—the deaths, the grief, the shedding of tears—were all part of a divine plan. "God has seen fit to visit us with the pestilence," he wrote his oldest son after the dysentery epidemic, "and Four of our number sleep in the dust."[7]

Brown raised his children according to strict Calvinistic rules. While he deplored the cruelties inflicted on slaves, he regularly beat his sons and daughters with a leather strap or a stick. His son John, Jr., claimed that his father kept what amounted to an account book to deal with his offenses: "For disobeying mother . . . eight lashes; For unfaithfulness at work . . . three lashes." One Sunday morning, John, Jr., was taken to the barn, where his father told him to remove his shirt because it was time to settle the account. Brown then struck his son on the bare back with a stout stick. But the father stopped at one third the number of strokes called for in the account book. Brown's next act astonished John, Jr., who explained: "Then father stripped off his shirt, and, seating himself on a block, gave me the stick and bade me 'lay it on' to his bare back. I dared not refuse to obey, but at first I did not strike hard. 'Harder!' he said. 'Harder, harder,' until he received the balance of the account."[8]

Though a profoundly religious man, John Brown rarely stayed loyal to any one church group. He argued with the parishioners or the church pastor over slavery and the treatment of blacks. Northerners on the frontier sometimes came to blows with each other over the slavery issue. Many favored slavery. Others simply hoped the institution would, in time, die out naturally.

Mary Brown, John Brown's second wife, posed for this photograph about 1851. On her left is daughter Annie, and on her right is daughter Sarah.

Still others demanded the abolition of slavery but did not want to live as equals with blacks.

Colonization societies were popular in the North. These societies urged the government to free the slaves and then ship them to Africa. In effect, the colonization societies wanted to stop slavery so that they could get rid of the nation's blacks.

Any wavering on the slavery issue infuriated John Brown. The suggestion that blacks and whites could not live as equals under one government also sent him into rages. He regularly invited blacks into his home to share his meals. He told his children the family should consider adopting a black orphan, although such an adoption never took place. At the time, free blacks in the North as well as in the South lived in separate and segregated communities. Many whites, even those opposed to slavery, thought of blacks as inferior. John Brown embraced blacks as equals in every respect, and this attitude often angered his neighbors and his fellow church members.

The Crusader

John Brown reached his fiftieth birthday in the year 1850. Because he was stoop-shouldered and looked older than his years, neighbors started calling him Old John Brown or simply Old Brown. He stood five foot ten. Thin, almost gaunt, his skin was leathery, and his face often bore a grim expression. When speaking about his love for God or his hatred of slavery, a mystical fire overcame him. One of his sons, Salmon, claimed, "His form and features attracted the attention of strangers quickly."[9] Another son said Brown looked as intimidating as a meat ax. Brown's most notable features were his intense eyes, which various people described as "hawklike" or "steely."

In business John Brown had been an utter failure. Over the course of his life he had attempted to earn a living as a tanner, a surveyor, a farmer, and a dealer in wool. Though he regularly worked twelve to fourteen

┌───┐
│   **SOURCE DOCUMENT**   │

THERE WERE A NUMBER OF FREE COLORED PERSONS AND
SOME FUGITIVE SLAVES [ATTENDING CHURCH SERVICES].
[THEY] WERE GIVEN SEATS BY THEMSELVES, NEAR THE
DOOR, NOT A GOOD PLACE FOR SEEING THE MINISTERS OR
SINGERS. FATHER NOTICED THIS, AND WHEN THE NEXT
MEETING HAD FAIRLY OPENED, HE ROSE AND CALLED
ATTENTION TO THE FACT, THAT, IN SEATING THE COLORED
PORTION OF THE AUDIENCE, A DISCRIMINATION HAD BEEN
MADE, AND SAID THAT HE DID NOT BELIEVE GOD IS "A
RESPECTER OF PERSONS." HE THEN INVITED THE COLORED
PEOPLE TO OCCUPY HIS SEAT. THE BLACKS ACCEPTED AND
OUR FAMILY TOOK THEIR VACATED SEATS. THIS WAS A BOMB-
SHELL. . . . NEXT DAY FATHER RECEIVED A CALL FROM THE
DEACONS TO ADMONISH HIM . . . BUT THEY RETURNED WITH
NEW VIEWS ON CHRISTIAN DUTY.[10]

└───┘

John Brown's eldest son, John Brown, Jr., described his father's reaction to racial discrimination at an Ohio church meeting in 1837.

hours a day, all his business enterprises collapsed. His family once suffered the humiliation of being forced out of a house by a local sheriff after failing to pay bank loans. According to Brown's Calvinistic beliefs, debt was to be avoided like sin itself. Yet John Brown almost never escaped the burden of debt in his adult years.

Brown led a double life as a businessman and an abolitionist. Many of his business pursuits allowed him to travel in the Northern states, where he met famous abolitionists such as Frederick Douglass and William

Lloyd Garrison. However, he never joined any of the abolitionist societies that then flourished in the North. As he had disagreed with the church groups, so he disagreed with the leadership and the goals of those societies. They were, in his opinion, made up of people who liked to talk too much. He wanted positive action, measures that were directly designed to break slavery's grip on the nation.

Just before he turned fifty, Brown had moved his family to North Elba, a settlement in the Adirondack Mountains of upstate New York. He built a farm on land donated to him by a wealthy abolitionist named Gerrit Smith. Already a free black community had developed in North Elba. More blacks passed through the region as Brown let it be known that his house was a station on the Underground Railroad. Brown dreamed of forming a society of free blacks and escaped slaves in upper New York State. From that society he would encourage Southern blacks to break free of bondage and unite in what would amount to a separate nation of North Elba.

As he aged, John Brown grew ever more militant in his personal crusade against slavery. He envisioned himself as a warrior commanded by God to attack and destroy that wicked institution. This soldier-of-God vision drove his thoughts and actions to operate in a realm above that of ordinary men. He believed a higher set of rules applied to a man answering God's call. If bloodshed were needed to eradicate a sin, so be it. God would smile on the spilled blood.

John Brown, from a picture taken in about 1850, when he was fifty years old.

To John Brown, the call for militancy was an order that thundered out of the heavens in the 1850s. It seemed the proslavery forces in America were growing in power with each evil act of the government—the Fugitive Slave Law, the *Dred Scott* decision, the Kansas-Nebraska Act. The last act, which permitted the opportunity for slavery to develop in the Kansas and Nebraska territories, was, for Brown, an invitation to war. He would go to Kansas. And he would go as an avenging angel, sword in hand, ready to smite all sinners who defamed the Lord.

A lasso might possibly be applied to a slave-catcher for once with good effect. Hold on to your weapons and never be persuaded to leave them. . . . Stand by one another and by your friends while a drop of blood remains; and be hanged if you must, but tell no tales. . . . Make no confession.

SOLDIER OF GOD

—John Brown's words of advice
to a militant antislavery group called the League of Gileadites, 1851[1]

Bleeding Kansas

To antislavery and proslavery Americans, the western territories loomed as a battleground. Those territories would be eligible to become states when they had a sufficient population. Would they enter the Union as slave states or free states? This question rocked the land in the 1850s. Two territories, Kansas and Nebraska, were rapidly filling up with settlers. In 1854 the United States Congress passed the Kansas-Nebraska Act, which allowed the settlers of the two territories to vote on whether or not they wanted slavery.

The Kansas-Nebraska Act infuriated antislavery Americans because slavery had been prohibited in the Kansas and Nebraska regions since 1820. Nebraska did not pose a problem to the antislavery forces, because its newly arriving settlers came mainly from the Northern states. But Kansas lay near Missouri, a slave state. From both Missouri and the Northern states, thousands of people spilled into Kansas. Many came not to settle but just to add their votes to their cause. And many came not to start farms but to fight.

Some historians claim that the first chapter of the Civil War broke out in Kansas in 1854. Starting that year, antislavery settlers formed a political group called the Free State party. Proslavery Missourians, whom many settlers called Border Ruffians, crossed into Kansas to oppose the Free Staters. Proslavery candidates won the Kansas elections of 1855, but Free Staters refused to accept the results of the elections. Day by day, tensions mounted. A dispute over farm boundaries between a proslavery and an antislavery settler led to a shoot-out. The shoot-out led to war. As many as two hundred people died in numerous small battles that raged between Free Staters and Border Ruffians. Newspapers began calling the territory "Bleeding Kansas."

The ultimate destiny of Kansas was sealed by the hundreds of antislavery settlers who poured into the territory each week. Although most of those settlers intended to stay in Kansas, the Missourians generally crossed over to the territory only to vote or to start trouble. The Free Staters soon held the majority in Kansas Territory. But the Border Ruffians were determined to commit one final, destructive act. In May

*Drawing of an 1858 battle fought in the Kansas Territory
between proslavery and antislavery forces.*

1856, a proslavery federal marshal led a band of eight hundred men into the town of Lawrence, Kansas. Lawrence was known as a hotbed of Free State activity. The small army degenerated into a mob. Homes were looted, a hotel was set on fire, and the printing presses of two antislavery newspapers were thrown into the Kaw River.

The sacking of Lawrence enraged Free Staters. In speeches and in a blizzard of pamphlets, the Free Staters called for revenge against the proslavery men. The loudest voice demanding revenge was that of John Brown, who believed he was God's special instrument for the destruction of slavery. Impatient with the timidity of most antislavery Americans, Brown was ready for war. To family and friends, Brown often repeated one of his favorite biblical passages, from Paul's Letter to the Hebrews, 9:22, ". . . everything is cleansed by blood and without the shedding of blood there is no forgiveness [of sin]."

Brown had arrived in Kansas about six months before the raid on Lawrence. He settled in the region of Osawatomie, joining four of his sons, who had come to Kansas about a year earlier. Brown's sons, now adults and independent thinkers, no longer shared John Brown's Calvinistic views on religion, but they were in perfect harmony with their father's antislavery passions.

The Brown family differed from the average Free Staters, who rejected slavery but still wanted nothing to do with black people. Many Free Staters favored

LIBERTY. THE FAIR MAID OF KANSAS_IN THE HANDS OF THE "BORDER RUFFIANS".

A drawing favored by Free State advocates called "Liberty, the Fair Maid of Kansas in the Hands of the 'Border Ruffians.'" The drawing predicted the ruin of Kansas if the Border Ruffians were allowed to take over the territory.

laws that barred blacks from even entering Kansas once it became a state. For the moment, Brown and his sons overlooked the prejudices of their Kansas neighbors. They concentrated on performing a special mission. They believed the Border Ruffians and the proslavery men had to be punished—and punished by the avenging hand of God.

The Pottawatomie Massacre

On the night of May 24, 1856, just three days after the destruction of Lawrence, John Brown and a band of seven men descended on the frontier town of Pottawatomie, Kansas. Included in the group were four of John Brown's sons and his son-in-law. They were armed with guns and heavy short-bladed swords, which they had honed to razor sharpness.

Following Pottawatomie Creek, the group approached the Doyle cabin. James Doyle and his sons were from Tennessee. They were leading proslavery men in the territory. John Brown knocked at the cabin door, pretending to be a lost traveler asking for directions. When Doyle answered, Brown shoved him inside. The band then stormed in, brandishing their guns and swords. Screams and commotion shook the cabin. Catching the murderous glint in John Brown's eyes, Mrs. Doyle pleaded for mercy. Ignoring her pleas, Brown ordered James Doyle and his sons outside. Mrs. Doyle cried out that at least her fourteen-year-old son should not be harmed. John Brown let the fourteen-year-old stay but pushed Doyle, his twenty-one-year-old son, and his twenty-year-old son out the door into the blackness of the night. There, not a hundred yards from the cabin door, Brown's group hacked the Doyle men to death with their swords. John Brown ordered the slayings and watched while the others did their grisly work.

Brown then marched his band half a mile down the creek to the cabin of Allen Wilkinson, another proslavery activist. This time Brown shouted out that he was the captain of the "Northern Army" and intended to take Wilkinson prisoner. Wilkinson's wife, who was gravely ill with the measles, sobbed piteously as the men dragged her husband toward the door.

Once outside they stabbed and cut Wilkinson with their swords.

Another cabin was visited that night by the Northern Army, and a proslavery settler named William Sherman was killed and mangled by Brown's swordsmen. Sherman's bloody body was thrown into Pottawatomie Creek.

Its mission completed, the Northern Army went home. History remembered the night of butchery as the Pottawatomie Massacre.

SOURCE DOCUMENT

WE THEN CROSSED THE POTTAWATOMIE, AND CAME TO THE HOUSE OF HENRY SHERMAN, GENERALLY KNOWN AS DUTCH HENRY. . . . THEY [THE GROUP] BROUGHT OUT WILLIAM SHERMAN, DUTCH HENRY'S BROTHER, MARCHED HIM DOWN INTO THE POTTAWATOMIE CREEK, WHERE HE WAS SLAIN WITH SWORDS, AND LEFT LYING IN THE CREEK. IT WAS THE EXPRESSED INTENTION OF JOHN BROWN TO EXECUTE DUTCH HENRY ALSO, BUT HE WAS FOUND NOT AT HOME. . . . I DESIRE TO SAY HERE THAT IT IS NOT TRUE THAT THERE WAS ANY INTENTIONAL MUTILATION OF THE BODIES AFTER THEY WERE KILLED. . . . I UNDERSTAND THAT THE KILLING WAS DONE WITH SWORDS SO AS TO AVOID ALARMING THE NEIGHBORHOOD BY THE DISCHARGE OF FIREARMS.[2]

James Townsley was a member of John Brown's group that committed the killings at Pottawatomie. His account of the murders appeared in the Lawrence, Kansas, Daily Journal *on December 10, 1879, more than twenty years after the event.*

Did John Brown at this point in his life believe the slaughter of five men would lead to the abolition of slavery? How could he, a devout Christian, sanction the merciless slayings? For more than one hundred years, Americans have puzzled over John Brown's thinking on the night of the massacre and his subsequent actions. Family members claimed that Brown was almost abnormally kind to animals. They said that although he was strict with his children, he was also loving—hugging them, telling stories, and singing little ones to sleep. Yet he ordered five unarmed men hacked to death with swords. Many historians have concluded that Brown was deranged on that horrible night in Kansas Territory. Perhaps Brown believed he was no longer a mortal man capable of sin. He was instead an arm of the Lord, a lightning bolt sent from the heavens to save his nation from evil.

Osawatomie Brown and His Grand Plan

Arrest warrants were issued for John Brown and his men, but in Bleeding Kansas there was no organized police force. After the killings, the Kansas Territory remained a land at war. In a battle at Black Jack Springs, Brown led a band of Free Staters to victory and earned the title "Captain" John Brown. However, Kansas was the scene of even further tragedy for the Brown family. In a skirmish near Osawatomie, John Brown's son Frederick was killed by a proslavery man's bullet. Shaking with grief and fury, Brown stood over Frederick's body and shouted to the sky,

"God sees it. I have only a short time to live—only one death to die, and I will die fighting for this cause. There will be no more peace in this land until slavery is done for."[3]

The nation's newspapers started calling him Osawatomie Brown or Captain Brown of Osawatomie. The killings of five proslavery men had made Brown the country's most famous abolitionist—or infamous, depending on one's point of view. Southern newspapers denounced Osawatomie Brown as a lunatic and a devil. Northern papers had a different view of the man and his well-publicized massacre. Some members of the Northern press claimed he killed the five in a fair fight; others said the massacre was the work of Indians; and still others wrote that the slayings did not occur at all. A reporter named James Redpath, who idolized Brown and visited him at Osawatomie, said, "I left [Brown's camp] with a far higher respect for the Great Struggle [against slavery] than ever I had felt before. . . . And I said, also, and thought, that I had seen the predestined leader of the second and the holier American Revolution."[4]

Shortly after his son was killed, Brown traveled through scores of Northern cities. There, he gave lectures on the evils of slavery. Before thrilled crowds, he gave stirring accounts of his actions in the guerrilla war taking place in Kansas. He was, of course, still a wanted man in the Kansas Territory. Now and then he was pursued by federal marshals who sought his arrest. Though Brown was an outlaw, cheering groups of antislavery men and women welcomed him into their churches and meeting halls. His role in the Pottawatomie Massacre—indeed the massacre itself—was rarely mentioned. Captain Brown of Osawatomie was greeted as a war hero, a fearless commander in a holy struggle.

The stated purpose of Brown's tour of the North was to raise money and to recruit an army to protect Free Staters in Kansas. But the flames of war dampened in the Kansas Territory by 1857. By then, Brown was quietly fashioning new plans to strike a bold and powerful blow against slavery.

Brown took the title of captain seriously. He began reading historic accounts of military commanders. He was especially interested in those generals who had built strongholds in the mountains and used those strongholds as a base to lash out at their enemies. Mountains, he concluded, are natural defensive works. On narrow and twisting mountain trails, ten well-placed men could hold off a hundred foes. Brown planned his moves like a general about to engage in battle. He pored over maps of the South, seeking a mountain fortress. Often his studies centered on western Virginia and the region where the Potomac and the Shenandoah rivers merge. In the heart of that region stood a town called Harpers Ferry.

To Brown, the course of his future grew clear, as if it were presented by God. Harpers Ferry was the site of a United States arsenal, where rifles were made and stored. With a small force of black and white soldiers, he would attack and capture Harpers Ferry in one lightning-like raid. He and his men would then carry all the firearms they could manage to the nearby mountains, where they would establish a fortress. Word of their attack on the arsenal would spread from Virginia to the other slave states. Answering the call of freedom, thousands of slaves would break away from their masters and join Brown in the mountains. There, using the captured firearms, Brown would form an army. Black and white freedom fighters from the North would bolster that army. This splendid force, charged with divine energy, would march out and crush slavery in the nation forever.

Brown needed time and money to execute his grand plan. For more than two years, he traveled the country, often stopping at Boston, to raise funds from abolitionists. When speaking to supporters, he was vague about his plans, explaining only that he intended to fight slavery. He did not want his idea of fomenting a mass slave uprising to leak out. Brown feared his scheme would shock those abolitionists who preached freedom but always stopped short of a fight. Such a man, Brown believed, was Wendell Phillips, a fiery speaker and writer for the abolitionist cause. Though he was considered heroic in abolitionist circles, Brown thought Phillips was too timid. Brown once wrote, "I have noticed that men who have the gift of eloquence. Such as our friend has, seldom are men of action; now it is men of action I wish to consult; and so you need say nothing to Wendell Phillips."[5]

After great effort Brown assembled a group of six men who were willing to give him money to emancipate the slaves. At first the six men knew few if any details about Brown's designs on Harpers Ferry. However, they were aware that they were giving money to a man wanted by the law, and therefore, they desired to keep their contributions secret. The group, which became known as the Secret Six, included Gerrit Smith, who had already provided Brown with his farm in North Elba; Thomas Wentworth Higginson, a minister and the editor of *Atlantic Monthly* magazine; Samuel Gridley Howe, a well known doctor; Theodore Parker, a minister; Franklin Sanborn, an educator; and George Luther Stearns, a businessman.

The Secret Six had a strange relationship with the militant abolitionist John Brown. As they learned details of his plans, the six urged him to return to Kansas and continue his antislavery activities there. This Brown refused to do. Then the six told him that under no circumstances should he reveal his ties to them. In effect, the Secret Six were willing to look the other way while John Brown waged a violent war against slavery, but they did not want to be directly connected to that war. In private conversations Brown sometimes denounced the Secret Six as weaklings. But he still took their money.

Assembling the Army of the Lord

Brown continued a relentless traveling schedule, picking up followers as he journeyed. In Tabor, Iowa,

Brown met Hugh Forbes, a British adventurer, whom he hired to be the drillmaster for his army. Brown led a raiding party into Missouri, where he freed eleven slaves, two of whom joined his forces. An Ohio schoolteacher named John Henry Kagi joined Brown. Kagi had few religious convictions, but he was dedicated to the emancipation of the nation's slaves. Brown eventually made Kagi his second in command.

In Connecticut Brown ordered an arms supplier to make a thousand short jabbing spears called pikes. He reasoned that the masses of slaves soon to join him in battle would be unschooled in the use of firearms. Therefore, the slaves would have to be armed with spears. Brown trusted that God would give his army of slaves the power needed to win battles despite its primitive weapons.

Though he made many moves, Brown believed his progress in gathering an army was agonizingly slow. The Secret Six sent him money reluctantly, and they never sent enough. Brown was uncertain whom to trust with details of his plans to raid Harpers Ferry. Many of his sympathizers were shocked by the boldness of the proposed raid and withdrew their support as soon as they learned the scope of Brown's intentions. Hugh Forbes, the drillmaster, grew angry at not being paid and told several important Northern politicians of the upcoming move on Harpers Ferry. Fortunately for Brown, the politicians did not take Forbes's warnings seriously. Many of those who heard of Brown's plans thought them too far-fetched to be believed and dismissed them as the dreamings of a madman.

Even Frederick Douglass, the runaway slave, told Brown that his attack was doomed to fail. Brown had first met Douglass in 1847. He often stayed at the Douglass home when traveling in New York. Brown admired the ex-slave as a heroic abolitionist, one willing to fight against the national evil. Yet when Brown informed Douglass of the intended raid, Douglass pleaded with him to drop his plans. Such a raid, said Douglass, would "array the whole country [and would be the same as] going into a perfect steel trap, and that once in [you would] never get out alive."[6] The meeting with Douglass left Brown disappointed but as determined as ever to proceed with his operation. He lamented that Douglass—who had felt the sting of the slave-master's whip—would shrink in the face of this grand opportunity to achieve emancipation.

Slowly Brown put together a small core of loyal followers. Five of his soldiers were black men. Dangerfield Newby, a former slave, wanted to fight for the freedom of his wife and seven children. Shields Green was once a follower of Frederick Douglass, but he left Douglass to join Brown's ranks. Another was a printer, and two others were students at Oberlin College in Ohio. Two of Brown's sons, thirty-four-year-old Owen and twenty-year-old Oliver, enlisted in the cause. A third son, Watson, joined the band weeks before the raid. Brown's son-in-law, William

Thompson, was a willing soldier. Also marching with Brown was twenty-six-year-old Jeremiah Anderson, whose grandfather was a Southern slave owner. Two Quaker brothers, Barclay and Edwin Coppoc, joined Brown's crusade. As members of the Quaker church, the Coppocs had taken vows never to fight and never to kill. Yet the brothers overlooked those vows to strike a blow against slavery.

In all, Brown's army totaled twenty-one men. This was a tiny force to fight all of Southern society. But numbers mattered little to John Brown. The warnings from his friends and supporters were also meaningless. He felt his venture was righteous and just. He would succeed because his mission had the blessing of God. His band of men also believed that, with God's help, they would triumph and shake the institution of slavery to its core.

Dangerfield Newby was one of five African Americans who served in John Brown's band. Newby had been freed by his master years earlier, but his wife and children were still held as slaves on a Virginia plantation.

In July 1859, Brown rented a farm in Maryland about five miles north of Harpers Ferry. Still running from the law, he signed the farm's lease, using the name Isaac Smith. He claimed to be a businessman from New York State who wanted to raise cattle. To further disguise his now familiar face, he grew a beard. Soon the beard became long and gray, giving him a patriarchal look, like a figure out of the Bible. A Cleveland, Ohio, newspaper reporter visited Brown at the Maryland farm and described him as "a compactly-built and wiry man, and as quick as a cat in his movements. His hair is of a salt and pepper hue and as stiff as bristles."[7] One feature on Brown's face that became even more prominent was his eyes. His eyes, always intense, now seemed to burn with a mystical fire.

Brown often walked to the heights to look down at the town of Harpers Ferry, Virginia. It was (and still is) a beautiful region of craggy hills and rushing rivers. Harpers Ferry had been established more than one hundred years earlier by Robert Harper, who ran a ferry business on the Shenandoah River. The arsenal there had been building guns for soldiers since the American Revolution. In Brown's time the town's population stood at roughly twenty-five hundred people. Of these, about one hundred fifty were free blacks and another one hundred fifty were slaves. Western Virginia was not a proslavery region. In fact, the west's resistance to slavery was a key issue in the forming of West Virginia as a free state in 1863. Still, Virginia was

A drawing of the town of Harpers Ferry as it appeared in 1859.

the South's intellectual and cultural leader. Harpers Ferry stood as a gateway in the mountains, a door that, if swung open, would allow escaping slaves to rush for freedom and join Brown's army.

"Men, get on your arms," John Brown announced in October 1859. "We will proceed to the Ferry."[8]

A dispatch just received from Frederick [Virginia] dated this morning states that an insurrection has broken out at Harpers Ferry where an armed band of Abolitionists has full possession of the government arsenal.

—The first news report of the raid on Harpers Ferry, received by the Associated Press office in Washington, D.C., at 7:45 A.M. on October 17, 1859[1]

5

JOHN BROWN'S RAID

The Armory Seized

A cold drizzle fell over Harpers Ferry on the night of October 16, 1859. John Brown led a group of eighteen men and a creaking wagon toward the lights of Harpers Ferry, Virginia. Three of his men remained at the Maryland farm to act as a rear guard. The wagon held two hundred rifles, two hundred pistols, and a thousand pikes. All these weapons were purchased with money from the Secret Six and a few other supporters. The arms were intended to be temporary supplies for the rebelling slaves until an even larger arsenal could be procured from the Harpers Ferry armory.

As the group drew near, two men branched off to cut telegraph lines leading into town. Then the band approached the nine-hundred-foot-long covered railroad bridge that spanned the Shenandoah River. That bridge was always guarded by a watchman. At the foot of the bridge, Brown nodded, and two men darted across. Wordlessly the two grabbed the watchman, who, at first, thought they were playing some sort of joke on him. But then, the watchman was brought before the deadly serious-looking John Brown and realized this was no joke. The watchman was taken prisoner.

Crossing the bridge, Brown and his men entered the streets of Harpers Ferry. It was a Sunday night. Lamps and candles flickered in the windows. Piano music came from the tavern at the Wager House Hotel. Only a few people walked the streets, and no one gave the band of men and their horse-drawn wagon a second glance.

Brown proceeded directly to the federal arsenal in the heart of the town. The arsenal building's watchman was also taken by surprise. To the terrified watchman, Brown announced, "I came here from Kansas; and this is a slave state; I want to free all the Negroes in this state; I have possession now of the United States armory, and if the citizens interfere with me I must only burn the town and have blood."[2]

Next, Brown's party seized several passersby as hostages. They then marched about half a mile up the road and took over Hall's Rifle Works, another storehouse of weapons. In less than an hour, Brown had captured rifles and ammunition worth more than a million dollars. He had enough weapons to supply a small army. It seemed as if, indeed, God had smiled on his plan.

Brown sent the wagon and several men to arrest Lewis W. Washington, the town's most prominent citizen. Washington, a slave owner and farmer, was the great-grandnephew of George Washington, the nation's first president. The wagon returned with a very frightened Lewis Washington aboard. He had been shaken awake and dragged out of bed in the middle of the night. Also in the wagon were ten "liberated" slaves. Three of the slaves belonged to Washington, and the others had been taken from a neighboring farm. Brown told Washington, "I wanted you particularly for the moral effect it would give our cause having one of your name our prisoner."[3] Brown gave the ten confused slaves pikes and ordered them to stand guard over the prisoners. Those slaves—all of whom had been forced off their farms—would be the only ones to join the great slave army of Brown's dreams.

The party that captured Lewis Washington also brought back a magnificent sword, the proudest possession in Washington's house. Tradition said the sword had been presented to George Washington by the European leader Frederick the Great. John Brown strapped the sword around his waist. Such a glittering weapon was an appropriate adornment for a triumphant general.

However, the glaring weaknesses of Brown's battle plans soon surfaced. No one had carried word of the

An 1859 cartoon, mocking John Brown's raid, was published in Harper's Weekly *magazine. It shows Brown giving a pike (spear) to a slave who is reluctant to accept the weapon.*

raid to the slave areas farther south. Therefore, the slave army that Brown envisioned never emerged. And for reasons that have always confounded historians, Brown seemed reluctant to leave Harpers Ferry. Within the first few hours of the raid, he commandeered an estimated one hundred thousand rifles and pistols and a sizable cache of ammunition. His second in command, John Kagi, urged him to carry the weapons to the mountains and establish a fortress as originally planned. But Brown waited. He later said he feared a flight from Harpers Ferry would trigger a gun battle, which could result in the hostages' being killed.

Initially, the raid at Harpers Ferry was bloodless and amazingly quiet. By midnight on October 16, the majority of Harpers Ferry residents were asleep in their beds, not even knowing their town was under siege by an abolitionist army.

The Battle Begins

Just after midnight a relief watchman named Patrick Higgins arrived at the Harpers Ferry bridge to serve his shift. He was promptly taken prisoner by two of Brown's men. But Higgins broke away, punching one of the raiders in the face in the process. The raiders fired their rifles. One bullet grazed Higgins on the side of the head. Still he managed to dash across the bridge and spread the alarm. The first shot in the battle of Harpers Ferry had been fired.

At about 1:20 A.M., a Baltimore and Ohio express train chugged toward Harpers Ferry en route to

Baltimore. By this time much of the town was aroused. Townspeople stopped the train as it approached the bridge and told the conductor that the bridge was being held by armed men. The train was packed with sleepy passengers who pressed their faces against the windows, wondering why they had made an unscheduled stop. In the darkness the train engineer and the conductor walked toward the bridge. They were stopped at gunpoint by the two abolitionist guards. At that moment, Hayward Shepherd, the baggage handler for Harpers Ferry station, also approached the bridge. When he saw a gunman, Shepherd turned and ran. A shot cracked in the night. Shepherd fell, badly wounded. He died in agony a short time later. Shepherd was a free black and a respected man among both blacks and whites in the community. How ironic that the first person killed at Harpers Ferry was an African American, gunned down in a battle designed to liberate his race.

Dawn broke over Harpers Ferry, now a town in terror. Everyone in the community milled about the streets. Stories of crime and atrocities spread by word of mouth, growing more horrific with each retelling. Hundreds of abolitionists had descended on the town, said the rumormongers. They had already freed thousands of slaves in the countryside. Rampaging slaves were at this very minute burning houses and killing people. Riders galloped out of Harpers Ferry to alert nearby towns. This very act—a mass slave uprising— was the South's most dreaded nightmare. Southerners

SOURCE DOCUMENT

THE INSURGENTS [AT HARPERS FERRY] HAVE BEEN TAKING
PERSONS FROM THIS SIDE OF THE RIVER, TYING THEM, AND
CARRYING THEM OFF AS SLAVES. THERE ARE NOW FROM
FIVE TO SEVEN HUNDRED WHITES AND BLACKS ENGAGED . . .
ALL THE PRINCIPAL CITIZENS [AT HARPERS FERRY] HAVE
BEEN IMPRISONED AND MANY OF THEM KILLED.[4]

*With the telegraph lines cut, reporters in the nation's
capital had no direct communication with Harpers
Ferry during John Brown's raid. The reporters relied
on rumors, innuendo, and pure make-believe to come
up with accounts such as this one, which appeared in
the* National Intelligencer *(a newspaper based in
Washington, D.C.) on October 18, 1859.*

feared slave rebellion with such horror that they rarely
even spoke of its possibility. Now it had happened at
Harpers Ferry, a storehouse of deadly weapons.

Meanwhile, Brown sat with his hostages, holed up
in the captured buildings. The man who fancied himself a military general seemed paralyzed with
indecision. Where were the bands of escaped slaves he
had counted on to expand his ranks? Blacks in the
Harpers Ferry community appeared to be as frightened and confused as the whites. As the sun rose,
white townsmen armed themselves with squirrel rifles,
knives, clubs, axes—any sort of weapon they could lay
their hands on. The bell on the town's Lutheran
church rang a frenzied alarm. Small militia units began

arriving from surrounding farms. Brown, not knowing what to do next, did nothing.

Men from the Charles Town militia charged the Potomac River bridge with their guns blazing and quickly chased away Brown's guards. Soon both bridges leading into town were held by militia forces, cutting off Brown's chances for withdrawal. Gunfire cracked and roared on the streets of Harpers Ferry as militia and townsmen worked to flush out the raiders.

The first of the raiders to fall from a militia bullet was Dangerfield Newby, the free black man who was fighting to liberate his wife and children from slavery. Newby was gunned down on the street. Folded in his pocket was a letter from his wife that said, "Oh dear Dangerfield come this fall. . . . I want to see you so much that is the one bright hope I have before me."[5] The victors showed no sympathy for their fallen foe. Furious townspeople beat Newby's body with sticks. One man cut off Newby's ears as souvenirs, and finally pigs were allowed to feed on his remains.

At the beginning of the raid, Brown made the mistake of dividing his already small band. He had men stationed at the Maryland farm, at the arsenal, and up the road at Hall's Rifle Works. Now Brown's tiny units within town were surrounded by militia forces that grew as the hours passed. Realizing that the opposition numbered fewer than twenty raiders, the town's defenders grew more confident and more hateful. Whiskey was passed freely among the Harpers Ferry defenders. The men broke into a roaring chant designed to terrify the raiders: *Kill them! Kill them! Kill them!*

Hall's Rifle Works was held by three of Brown's men, led by John Kagi. With the building under constant rifle fire, the men tried to escape. Kagi fled from the back door, raced toward the Potomac River, and attempted to wade across. He was shot in the head and died instantly. The two others, Lewis Leary and John Copeland, were captured. Both Leary and Copeland were free blacks who had enlisted in John Brown's army months earlier. To the white townsmen, they were the symbol of dread—blacks with guns. Mobs wanted to lynch the two on the spot, but Leary and Copeland were saved by a Harpers Ferry doctor who urged the enraged people to let the law handle the matter. Leary, who had been shot in the chest, died that night.

John Brown sent a hostage and his son-in-law, William Thompson, out with a white flag of truce. He hoped to secure safe conduct for himself and his raiders to get out of town in exchange for the release of the hostages. The crowd ignored the white flag and carried Thompson away. Brown next took eleven of his most important hostages and barricaded himself and his remaining soldiers in the town's firehouse. That engine house became known as Fort Brown. From the beginning, however, it was a fort under siege.

Twenty-year-old Billy Leeman, the youngest of Brown's followers, became rattled by the chants, fury, and drunkenness of the crowd. From the armory yard he made a desperate run for his life. Leeman was

The engine house called "Fort Brown," where Brown, his
soldiers, and his hostages took refuge. Since the raid, the
building has had an unusual history. In 1892 it was
disassembled and moved to Chicago to serve as an exhibit
for that city's World Fair. From 1909 to 1968, it stood at
Storer College, a predominantly black school in Harpers
Ferry. The building now stands on the riverbank near its
original location.

wounded by a bullet and threw his hands in the air to surrender. A local man approached to within a few feet of him and shot him in the face with a pistol. Leeman's body was then used for target practice by a dozen or so militia riflemen.

Once more, Brown tried for a truce and sent out a party of three men waving a white flag. This time, the flag was carried by his son Watson. The militia force surrounding the engine house allowed the party to step into full sight, and then opened fire. A bullet tore into Watson Brown's stomach. He staggered back to the engine house, screaming in pain. Clearly, no gentlemanly rules of war would hold sway in this conflict.

In the late afternoon a shot rang out of the engine house and killed Fontaine Beckham, the mayor of Harpers Ferry. Beckham, a kindly older man, was known and liked throughout the community. Earlier he had tried to quell the temper of the crowd and to curb their drinking. Now, with Beckham's death, whiskey flowed and anger boiled anew. A dozen men led by a saloon keeper turned on their one raider prisoner, William Thompson, the husband of Brown's daughter Ruth. The men pushed and kicked Thompson down the street to the banks of the Potomac. Near the railroad bridge Thompson faced the mob and shouted, "You may kill me, but it will be revenged. There are eighty thousand persons sworn to carry out this work."[6] Men in the crowd shot him with pistols, and he fell into the shallow waters. Witnesses claimed Thompson's body could be seen lying face up for the next two days, his expression mirroring the horror of his death.

Washington Reacts

Word of the Harpers Ferry battle blazed across the countryside and soon reached Washington, D.C., some sixty miles to the southeast. Rumors and exaggerated stories told of a slave uprising that had struck in western Virginia. According to the wild accounts, hundreds of slaves were burning buildings, looting stores, and killing everyone in their path. The stories further claimed that armies of slaves and abolitionists were marching toward the nation's capital. The mayor of Washington called out the police force and stationed guards at all roads leading into town. Many Washingtonians fled the town in terror.

In the White House, President James Buchanan heard the reports from Harpers Ferry. The latest word claimed that the abolitionist army besieging the town totaled seven hundred whites and freed slaves, all well armed. Buchanan, who was from Pennsylvania, had been attempting to hold the country together amid the exploding arguments over slavery. He was a fence-sitter, reluctant to side with either the North or the South. To Northerners, he was a disappointment. The president, though he tried to avoid upsetting either side, took a proslavery position on important issues such as the Kansas problem and the *Dred Scott* decision. To deal with the insurrection at Harpers Ferry, Buchanan sent three artillery companies and a unit of ninety marines to the town. To command these forces, the president chose a brilliant army colonel named Robert E. Lee and ordered him to put down the rebellion as quickly as possible.

Robert E. Lee came from one of Virginia's most important families. Though a Southerner, he was against slavery. He often said slavery was a great evil both to the slaves and to their masters. As a young man, Lee freed the slaves he inherited from his family. Honor and duty were the keystones in his life. When President Buchanan ordered him to suppress the insurrection at Harpers Ferry, Lee prepared to do just that in an efficient military manner. For his second in command, Lee selected fellow Virginian Lieutenant James Ewell Brown "Jeb" Stuart. Within two years, Lee and Stuart would electrify the nation with their bold moves as leaders of the Southern armies during the Civil War.

As Lee and his forces rushed toward Harpers Ferry, the town suffered through a tense, violent night. Brown, his men, and his hostages remained in the engine house. Outside, hundreds of militiamen and townsmen—many of whom were drunk—swirled through the streets. The arsenal and the tavern had been open all night. Anyone who wanted a rifle and whiskey got them. The town's defenders were reluctant to charge the engine house because Brown's gunmen were crouched behind the windows, aiming their rifles onto the streets. Militia leaders also worried that the abolitionists would kill their hostages. Unable to act, the defenders stood about in groups, drinking,

Robert E. Lee (1807–1870) commanded the unit sent to subdue John Brown and his raiders and later led the Southern armies in the Civil War.

chanting, shouting threats to the raiders, and firing their rifles into the air. One townsman named Patrick Higgins remembered, "The people kept shouting and shouting at random and howling."[7]

With his soldiers, Robert E. Lee arrived at Harpers Ferry in the early-morning hours of October 18. At first, Lee did not know that the leader of the raiders was the notorious John Brown of Osawatomie, Kansas. However, the name and reputation of his adversary made little difference to Lee. He had been given a task by the president, and he intended to fulfill his mission.

Assault on Fort Brown

By midnight the raiders were still inside the engine house, all of them weary without food or sleep. Brown's sons Watson and Oliver had suffered agonizing stomach wounds and lay near death. Brown paced about in the darkness of the tiny room. He still wore the sword commandeered from Lewis Washington's house.

Despite the gloomy circumstances, John Brown's face was a mask of determination. Lewis Washington, the most prominent prisoner, later said Brown was "the coolest and firmest man I ever saw."[8] In one corner, Brown's son Oliver clutched his bleeding belly and cried out, "Oh God, let me die, let me die." Brown said, "Be quiet, son. If you must die, die like a man." Then, after a few minutes of silence, Brown called out,

"Oliver, Oliver." There was no answer. "I guess he is dead," said John Brown.[9]

It was seven in the morning on Tuesday, October 18, when Lieutenant Jeb Stuart approached the engine house. He waved a white flag and gestured that he was coming in peace. Still, all parties knew flags of truce were not recognized in this battle. Stuart took a daring chance when he walked to the door of the engine house alone. Already he was displaying the brand of bravery that would make him the most feared of all cavalry commanders in the coming Civil War.

At the door Stuart recognized the raider chief and said, "I know you, you are Osawatomie Brown. I met you in Kansas." Stuart had encountered Brown in Kansas when Stuart commanded an army unit trying to stop the settler war in that territory. Brown leaned close to the door and said, "Yes, I did my duty there [in Kansas]."[10]

Standing stiffly outside the door, Stuart then produced a piece of paper and read a formal request for surrender written by his commander:

Colonel Lee, United States army, commanding the troops sent by the President of the United States to suppress the insurrection at this place, demands the surrender of the persons in the armory building. If they will peacefully surrender themselves . . . they will be kept in safety to await the orders of the President.[11]

Behind Stuart stood ranks of marines holding rifles with fixed bayonets. A few marines carried sledgehammers. If Brown did not surrender—and both Lee

James Ewell Brown "Jeb" Stuart (1833–1864), served as Lee's assistant during the Harpers Ferry battle and then became a feared cavalry commander for the armies of the South in the Civil War.

and Stuart assumed the raider leader would refuse to give up—the marines were to storm forward and break down the engine-house door.

A conversation began between Brown and Stuart. Brown reiterated his desire to be escorted out of town before he released his prisoners. Stuart said Brown must surrender with no preconditions. Finally Stuart asked, "Are you ready to surrender and trust to the mercy of the government?" Brown answered, "No, I prefer to die here."[12] At that point, Stuart stepped to the side and waved his hat. This was a prearranged signal for the marines to charge. The assault on "Fort Brown" began.

Three marines raced forward and began battering the engine-house door with sledgehammers. Brown's men tried to shoot at the marines, but withering rifle fire kept the raiders pinned down behind windows. For a few desperate minutes, the marines pounded away at the thick door with little effect. The crowd cheered, thoroughly enjoying the show. Next, a group of marines seized a ladder and used it as a battering ram—once, twice, and finally on the third time the door caved in.

In burst the marines. Two raiders were bayoneted to death. Lieutenant Israel Green, leader of the marine detachment, cornered the bearded leader of the raiders. In his haste to leave Washington, D.C., the lieutenant had strapped on his dress sword, the one he wore during parades, instead of his regular combat sword. No matter, Green stabbed Brown in the stomach with the dull sword and hit him over the head with the handle. The bearded man collapsed, badly wounded.

The assault on Fort Brown was over in less than three minutes. A writer from *Harper's Weekly* magazine watched the battle and wrote, "The dead and dying outlaws were dragged out onto the lawn amidst the howls and execrations of the people. It was a hideous and ghastly spectacle."[13] One of the raiders dying of his wounds was Watson Brown, one of John Brown's sons. A Baltimore reporter asked Watson what had motivated him to attack Harpers Ferry. "Duty, sir," he replied. The reporter worked for a proslavery newspaper, but he was nonetheless impressed by the courage

Marines storming Fort Brown, as depicted by an artist in an 1859 drawing in Frank Leslie's Illustrated *magazine.*

John Brown's capture is depicted in this drawing from Frank
Leslie's Illustrated.

the raiders had shown. He gave Watson a cup of water and asked whether he thought it was within his duty to shoot people. Watson replied, "I am dying. I cannot discuss the question. I did my duty as I saw it."[14]

A few hours later, Watson Brown died of his wounds.

His [John Brown's] zeal in the cause of my race was far greater than mine. . . . I could live for the slave, but he could die for him.

—Frederick Douglass[1]

6

SLAVERY ON TRIAL

The Aftermath of John Brown's Raid

John Brown's raid on Harpers Ferry lasted thirty-six hours, from the time he and his men crossed the Potomac River bridge to his capture at the hands of Robert E. Lee and the marines. Seventeen men had been killed: ten raiders (including two of Brown's sons), four townsmen, two of the slaves who had been forced to join Brown's band, and one marine. Four of Brown's followers—Aaron Stevens, Edwin Coppoc, Shields Green, and John Copeland—were captured, and four escaped. One of the escapees was Owen Brown, the son who had been assigned to guard the farmhouse and did not participate in the Harpers Ferry battle. Owen was never arrested; he died in 1889 at the age of sixty-five.

The wounded commander of the raid was temporarily imprisoned in an office next to the engine house. There, his wounds were dressed, and he talked calmly with his captors. Though blood still stained his clothes, hands, and beard, the raider chief granted an interview with reporters and others that lasted three hours. The interview was written up and published in just about all the nation's major newspapers. One of the men who questioned the country's most famous prisoner was Henry Wise, the governor of Virginia:

QUESTION: Can you tell us, who furnished the money for your expedition?

JOHN BROWN: I furnished most of it myself. I cannot implicate others. It is by my own folly that I have been taken. . . .

QUESTION: But you killed some people [here].

JOHN BROWN: Well, sir, if there was anything of that kind done it was done without my knowledge. . . .

QUESTION: What was your object in coming?

JOHN BROWN: We came to free the slaves, and only that. . . .

QUESTION: How do you justify your acts?

JOHN BROWN: I think you [the Southern states] are guilty of a great wrong against God and humanity—I say it without wishing to be offensive—and it would be perfectly right for any one to interfere with you so far as to free those you willfully and wickedly hold in bondage. . . .

QUESTION: Upon what principal do you justify your acts?

JOHN BROWN: Upon the Golden Rule. I pity the poor in bondage that have none to help them. That is why I am here. . . .

QUESTION: Who are your advisers in this movement?

JOHN BROWN: I cannot answer that. . . . I want you to understand that I respect the rights of the poorest and weakest colored people, oppressed by the slave system, just as much as I do those of the most wealthy and powerful. This is the idea that has moved me and that alone. . . .[2]

In this interview Brown established a pattern he would later use at his trial. First, he would say little about his financial backers, such as the Secret Six. Second, he would insist that slavery, not he, was the guilty party in the Harpers Ferry episode.

While he spoke, the mood of townspeople in Harpers Ferry grew uglier. A chorus of shouts roared

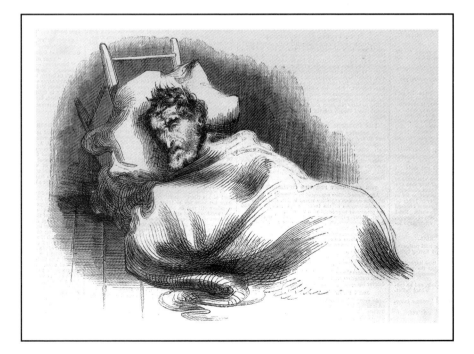

A drawing from Harper's Weekly *magazine shows the wounded John Brown after the raid.*

out: "Lynch him!" and "The scaffold is going up."[3] Fearing disorder, Colonel Lee decided to move Brown and the four other prisoners. Under heavy guard, Brown and the others were taken to Charles Town, some eight miles southwest of Harpers Ferry. There, within a week, the most important American trial thus far in the nineteenth century would begin.

The Nation in Shock

In every corner of the United States, newspapers blared the story of Harpers Ferry. The siege of the Virginia town was the talk of the country. For decades, the explosive issue of slavery had gathered on the horizon like a summer storm bound to strike. Now, the storm had roared over the nation, and Old Brown—Osawatomie Brown—was its thunder and lightning. Brown was a savior in some sections of the country and a devil in others. Every American had an opinion.

Upon the Southern states, the raid had an electric effect. The unthinkable had taken place. A Northern white man, backed by Northern money, had come to the South to foment a slave revolution. The South demanded that John Brown be punished for his evil act. Southern newspapers led the frenzy. The Mobile, Alabama, *Register* said, "For the first time the soil of the South has been invaded and its blood has been shed upon by armed abolitionists [who] invoked our slaves to rebellion."[4] The Albany, Georgia, *Patriot* cried out, "An undivided South says let [John Brown] hang!"[5]

Fear of more abolitionist attempts to excite slave rebellion swept the South. In the days after the raid, every Southern state increased its militia forces. Within weeks Virginia had four thousand men under arms. Other Southern states put out the call for volunteers. In fact, the Southern armies, which fought so bravely in the Civil War, were founded largely in the aftermath of Harpers Ferry.

At first, most Northerners seemed confused by the actions of John Brown. If he really wanted to provoke a slave uprising, why did he strike at an area where there were so few slaves? And why did he not send word of his mass insurrection to the plantations, where there were thousands of slaves who might have been willing to join his movement? Some Northern newspapers indicated that John Brown was a madman who deserved pity more than punishment.

But Northern intellectuals and poets, who had condemned the South for years, praised the bold scope of Brown's attempt to free the slaves. In the weeks and months after the raid, abolitionist writers hailed John Brown as a great liberator. Ralph Waldo Emerson said that if Brown were to hang, he "will make the gallows glorious like the Cross."[6] Poet William Dean Howells pictured his hero John Brown, wounded in battle and held captive in a Virginia jail, and wrote:

Old lion! tangled in the net,
Baffled and spent, and wounded sore,
Bound, thou who ne'er knew bonds before:
A captive, but a lion yet.[7]

John Brown on Trial

Initially, law enforcement officials pondered a tricky legal question: Brown's raid occurred on Virginia soil, but he attacked an arsenal owned by the federal government. Given this set of circumstances, should he be tried in a federal or a state court? Governor Wise solved the problem by insisting that Brown go to trial in Virginia and by Virginia courts. He reasoned that a state trial would be speedier and a verdict of guilty would be more certain than if the prisoner were turned over to the federal court system. The governor knew a guilty verdict and a quick execution would enhance his political career. President James Buchanan, who had no desire to offend the South, allowed the trial to take place in Virginia.

On the morning of October 25, 1859, just one week after their capture, Brown and his four captured raiders were taken from the jail and moved across the street to the Jefferson County Courthouse. The prosecutor read a long list of charges: treason against Virginia, murder, and conspiring with slaves to rebel. Brown and the others pleaded "not guilty" to all charges. If found guilty of any one of the offenses, the raiders could be given the death penalty. The court granted each of the five men separate trials. John Brown, the raider chief, would be tried first.

Brown's trial began on October 27. Brown claimed that the injuries he suffered during the raid made it impossible for him to stand on his feet for long periods of time. Therefore, through most of the trial, he lay on a cot. Yet to many observers, Brown's injuries did not seem to be particularly severe. Certainly the prisoner had not lost the fire in his eyes. A New York *Herald* reporter observed, "His confinement has not at all tamed the daring of his spirit."[8]

In the opening moments of his trial, the judge asked Brown whether he had a lawyer to defend him. Brown shouted like a preacher at a pulpit,

> Virginians! Virginians! I did not ask for quarter at the time I was taken. I did not ask that my life be spared. . . . If you seek my blood you may have it at any moment without the mockery of a trial. I have had no council. I have not been able to advise with anyone. I am ready for my fate. I do not ask a trial.[9]

John Brown hears evidence during his trial. This picture was sketched for Frank Leslie's Illustrated *magazine.*

Despite Brown's outburst the judge assigned two lawyers to defend the accused. The lawyers asked for a delay to allow Brown to recover fully from his wounds. This the judge denied. The trial must proceed at once. Then Brown's lawyers tried another tactic. The lawyers, acting without his approval, claimed that Brown was insane and, therefore, not accountable for his actions. The defense team suggested that Brown's mother, who had died in grief after the death of her baby daughter, was herself mad and had passed that affliction on to her son. The attorneys pleaded with the judge to confine Brown to a hospital rather than send him to the gallows.

Upon hearing this insanity plea, Brown waved his fist in the air and struggled on his cot to a sitting position. "If the court will allow me [to speak]," he shouted.[10] The judge granted him permission to state his mind. Brown declared he was not a madman:

> Insane persons, as far as my experience goes, have but little ability to judge of their own insanity, and if I am insane, of course I should think that I know more than all the rest of the world. But I do not think so. I am perfectly unconscious of insanity and I reject so far as I am capable any attempt to interfere with me on that score.[11]

With the insanity plea dismissed, the trial continued to the next day. The presiding judge, Richard Parker, hoped to conclude the trial speedily because he feared mobs would break into the Charles Town jail and lynch his prisoner. The judge had also heard rumors, some of which had validity, that gangs of abolitionists were plotting to rescue Brown from his jail cell.

In the North most of Brown's financial supporters lived in fear because of their own involvement in the raid. In theory the members of the Secret Six, who had given Brown money to carry out the Harpers Ferry operation, could also face the gallows if Brown were convicted. A vengeful South delighted in the prospect of rooting out the wealthy men who had funded Brown's act of treason. Several members of the Secret Six went into hiding. Only Thomas Higginson, the magazine publisher and Boston minister, stood his ground. Higginson boasted about his ties to John Brown and defied Virginia authorities to arrest him. He also made plans to rescue John Brown from jail, but he was never able to carry them out. The Secret Six were saved from prosecution largely because Brown refused to talk about the group's involvement with the raid.

Over the next two days, Brown said little in his own defense. In fact, witnesses claimed he sometimes dozed off while lying on his cot. But in his mind Brown had a dramatic speech prepared and was waiting for the proper moment to deliver it to the court. Behind the scenes he argued with his lawyers and was quick to dismiss them. In all, five different lawyers worked on Brown's case. One lawyer, George Hoyt, had been sent to Charles Town by Brown's Northern friends, who were plotting an escape attempt. Hoyt was to serve as a spy and report on the whereabouts of Brown's jail cell and the number of guards assigned to

SOURCE DOCUMENT

THEY ARE THEMSELVES MISTAKEN WHO TAKE HIM TO BE A MADMAN. HE IS A BUNDLE OF THE BEST NERVES I EVER SAW. . . . HE IS A MAN OF CLEAR HEAD, OF COURAGE, FORTITUDE, AND SIMPLE INGENUOUSNESS. HE IS COOL, COLLECTED, AND INDOMITABLE, AND IT IS BUT JUST TO HIM TO SAY THAT HE WAS HUMANE TO HIS PRISONERS. . . . COLONEL WASHINGTON [BROWN'S PRISONER] SAYS THAT HE WAS THE COOLEST AND FIRMEST MAN HE EVER SAW IN DEFYING DANGER AND DEATH. WITH ONE SON DEAD BY HIS SIDE AND ANOTHER SHOT, HE FELT THE PULSE OF HIS DYING SON WITH ONE HAND, HELD HIS RIFLE WITH THE OTHER, AND [STILL] COMMANDED HIS MEN WITH THE UTMOST COMPOSURE.[12]

During the trial, Virginia Governor Henry Wise displayed a grudging admiration for Brown's heroic duty to his cause. In a written statement, Wise also dismissed any notion that the prisoner was insane.

him. The escape plan, however, was deemed too risky and was never acted upon.

John Brown tried to delay the court proceedings and stretch the trial over many days. He wanted a long trial, not because he feared the outcome, but because he knew the eyes of the nation were focused on the tiny Virginia courthouse. Like a modern politician, Brown understood the value of publicity and the power of newspaper headlines. He had long before given himself up for dead. Now he wanted to put a price on his death. By becoming a martyr to the anti-slavery cause, he would strike a fatal blow to the institution he despised. John Brown's mission was to switch the focus of the proceedings and put slavery—instead of John Brown—on trial.

As the trial continued, a dozen witnesses testified to the violence of the raid. The hostages, including Lewis Washington, told their stories. Brown—as a delay tactic—argued that he was a general fighting a war and ought to be tried by rules of war rather than in a local court like a common criminal. The request for a military trial was denied by the judge. The jury, all local men, listened in rapt attention.

The trial lasted three and a half days. Finally, on the afternoon of October 31, lawyers on both sides made their closing arguments. The jury withdrew, discussed the case for forty-five minutes, and returned. Their verdict: John Brown was guilty of all three charges against him—murder, treason, and encouraging a slave rebellion. A strange hush gripped the courtroom. "Not the slightest sound was heard in the vast crowd as this verdict was heard and read," wrote one witness. "Not the slightest expression of elation or triumph was uttered from the hundreds present, who, a moment before, outside the court, joined in heaping threats upon [John Brown's] head."[13] Especially quiet and seemingly unmoved was John Brown. One reporter claimed Brown was intent on picking his teeth with a toothpick during the reading of the verdict.

On November 2, Brown was returned to court for sentencing. Before passing sentence, the judge asked Brown whether he had anything to say to the court.

This was Brown's glorious moment. He knew every newspaper in the country would carry his speech. It was as if the nation were leaning forward to catch his every word.

"This court acknowledges, as I suppose, the validity of the law of God," Brown said to the tense courtroom.

> I see a book kissed here which I suppose to be the Bible, or at least the New Testament. That teaches me that all things whatsoever I would that men should do to me, I should do even so to them. It teaches me even further to "remember them that are in bonds, as bound with them." I endeavored to act up to that instruction. . . . I believe that to have interfered as I have done—as I have always freely admitted I have done—in behalf of His despised poor, was not wrong,

John Brown rose from his cot to address the court.

but right. Now, if it is deemed necessary that I should forfeit my life for the furtherance of the ends of justice, and mingle my blood further with the blood of my children and with the blood of millions in this slave country whose rights are disregarded by wicked, cruel, and unjust enactments—I submit; so let it be done![14]

Brown's speech to the Virginia court became a classic in antislavery literature. It was read by millions in the North. The Lawrence, Kansas, *Republican* compared it to Holy Scripture: "For sublimity and solemn appeal, [Brown's speech] has not been excelled since Paul spoke before King Agrippa."[15] Years later, schoolchildren in some Northern communities were required to memorize and recite long passages of John Brown's address before the Charles Town, Virginia, court.

Judge Parker sentenced John Brown to hang. The execution was to take place on December 2, 1859, at a field outside of Charles Town. The four other raider prisoners were also tried and sentenced to the gallows. Fittingly, Old John Brown—their leader—was slated to die first.

Virginia today is . . . a pirate ship. John Brown sails with letters . . . from God and justice against every pirate he meets. He has twice as much right to hang Governor Wise as Governor Wise has to hang him.

—Abolitionist leader Wendell Phillips, speaking on the day the Virginia court condemned John Brown to death[1]

★ 7 ★

THE DEATH AND LEGACY OF JOHN BROWN

A Martyr Goes to the Gallows

"My dear children," John Brown wrote from his jail cell ten days before his execution date,

> I bless God that He has enabled you to bear the heavy tidings of our disaster with so much seeming resignation and composure of mind. That is exactly the thing I have wished you all to do for me—to be cheerful and perfectly resigned to the holy will of a wise and good God. . . . A calm peace . . . seems to fill my mind by day and by night. . . . Do not, my dear children, any of you grieve for a single moment on my account. As I trust my life has not been thrown away, so I also humbly trust my death will not be in vain.[2]

His jailers agreed with the theme of the letter. Brown appeared content, even happy, as he waited for his date with the gallows. He wrote endless letters and received visitors. He spoke softly to his jail guards, even those who argued with him over his antislavery views. Brown's courage in facing death served as an inspiration to the other raider prisoners who were held in adjoining cells. All became determined to go to the gallows in the spirit of their leader, knowing that their deaths were meaningful. From his jail cell, the African-American college student John Copeland wrote his parents, "I am not terrified by the gallows. Could I die in a more noble cause? Could I die in a manner and for a cause which would induce true and honest men more to honor me, and the angels more ready to receive me to their happy home of everlasting joy above?"[3]

The night before Brown's scheduled execution, the jailer brought John Brown a special visitor—Mary Brown, his wife. She wept. For the first time since his confinement, John Brown shed tears, too. Quickly, they both recovered and spoke of everyday matters such as the health of the children and the condition of their New York farm. Brown wanted to spend his last night with his wife, but the chief guard said that was impossible. With an embrace, John and Mary Brown parted. The condemned man passed the night writing letters and reading his Bible. He even managed to get a few hours' sleep.

Just before eleven in the morning on December 2, 1859, John Brown was led past the other cells toward the jailhouse door. "Stand up like men," he told his fellow raiders, "and do not betray your friends." One

SOURCE DOCUMENT

IN PURSUANCE OF INSTRUCTIONS FROM THE GOVERNOR, NOTICE IS HEREBY GIVEN TO ALL WHOM IT MAY CONCERN: THAT, AS HERETOFORE, PARTICULARLY FROM NOW UNTIL AFTER FRIDAY NEXT THE 2ND OF DECEMBER, STRANGERS FOUND WITHIN THE COUNTY OF JEFFERSON AND COUNTIES ADJACENT, HAVING NO KNOWN AND PROPER BUSINESS HERE, AND WHO CANNOT GIVE SATISFACTORY ACCOUNT OF THEMSELVES, WILL AT ONCE BE ARRESTED. . . .[4]

While John Brown calmly waited for death, the western Virginia countryside was aflame with fear that bands of abolitionists were ready to rescue the raider from jail. To prevent unrest, Governor Henry Wise printed hundreds of copies of this proclamation and nailed them on trees and buildings.

raider prisoner, Aaron Stevens, shouted, "Good-by, Captain. I know you are going to a better land." Brown replied, "I know I am."[5]

Outside, a clear, bright morning greeted Brown and his guards. It was unusually warm for early December. Soldiers lined the streets. Ranks of men bearing rifles stretched to the place of execution, a field not a five-minute walk from the courthouse. Though his arms were tied behind his back at the elbows, Brown managed to hand a guard a note. The complete note (the emphasis is his) read: "I John Brown am now quite *certain* that the crimes of this *guilty, land*: *will* never be purged *away*; but with Blood.

I had *as I now think*; *vainly* flattered myself that without *very much* bloodshed; it might be done."[6]

Brown boarded a horse-drawn wagon. There, he sat for the brief ride to the execution site on what was to be his coffin. Since seven in the morning, carpenters had been hammering together a scaffold and gallows, which now stood in a field just outside the small town. The rope to be used for the hanging had been on public display for all to gape at for the previous three days. However, the general public was forbidden to attend the execution because authorities feared a riot would break out.

A guard consisting of hundreds of officers and other men witnessed the hanging. Most prominent among the soldiers was a company of cadets from the Virginia Military Institute. The company was led by a stern-faced professor named Thomas J. Jackson. Later called Stonewall Jackson, he became one of the South's greatest military commanders in the Civil War. Standing in the ranks of another guard unit was a handsome twenty-one-year-old part-time soldier who bitterly hated all abolitionists. He was a promising actor named John Wilkes Booth. Five and a half years later, at the end of the Civil War, Booth would secretly enter a theater box occupied by President Abraham Lincoln and shoot the president in the head, killing him.

If Booth and other proslavery men hoped to see a whimpering and repentant John Brown, they were disappointed. Brown was marched up the steps of the gallows and stood, stiff as a statue, awaiting his fate. A prominent Virginia plantation owner named Edmund Ruffin noted, "[John Brown's] movements and manner gave no evidence of being either terrified or concerned and he went through what was required of him apparently with as little agitation as if he had been the willing assistant instead of the victim."[7]

A white hood was placed over John Brown's head, and he was directed to stand on a trapdoor. His ankles were tied together. A guard slipped the noose over his head and around his neck. Then confusion delayed the proceedings as officers argued who should stand where during the actual hanging. "Be quick," said John Brown from behind his hood.[8] Those were his last words. A soldier sprung the trap, and John Brown was hanged.

John Brown ascending the gallows, from an 1859 engraving that appeared in Frank Leslie's Illustrated.

Soldiers watched Brown's lifeless body swing slowly. An almost frightening hush engulfed the field. Finally, the voice of a militia commander broke the stillness: "So perish all such enemies of Virginia! All such enemies of the Union! All such enemies of the human race!"[9]

Reflections on John Brown

Was John Brown a madman? Was he a devil? Was he a saint? Then and now Americans argue about the character of John Brown. In fact, many debates about John Brown touch upon issues that are as modern as today. For example, say a person today lives in a nation that— so the person believes—denies human rights to his or her ethnic group. The person throws a bomb into a crowded public place. Victims call the bomb-thrower a terrorist, a cold-hearted murderer who uses a political cause to mask a desire to spill blood. But members of the despairing ethnic group hail the bomb-thrower as a freedom fighter, someone willing to risk imprisonment and death in order to liberate his or her people. This clash of outlooks—freedom fighter versus terrorist—differs little from the arguments that raged some one hundred fifty years ago over the man and cause of John Brown.

In Kansas, Brown murdered five men. The victims held proslavery views, but none of them owned slaves at the time. Southerners denounced Brown as a brutal slayer, but firebrand abolitionists chose to ignore the Kansas killings and focus on John Brown, the warrior for emancipation. In contrast, coolheaded antislavery Americans worried that Brown—though his cause was just—acted in a reckless and violent manner. Many slavery foes regarded Brown as an embarrassment to their movement. Salmon P. Chase, a prominent member of the newly formed Republican party, said of Brown and his raid, "Poor old man. How sadly misled by his own imaginations. How rash—how mad—how criminal then to stir up insurrection which if successful would deluge the land with blood and make void the fairest hopes of mankind."[10] The most important Republican of the time was Abraham Lincoln of Illinois. Lincoln was not an abolitionist. Instead, he hoped that slavery would simply fade away like a bad dream. Speaking on the night of John Brown's execution, Lincoln said, "We cannot object [to the execution], even though he agreed with us in thinking that slavery is wrong. That cannot excuse violence, bloodshed, and treason."[11]

Religious groups struggled with the moral questions posed by Brown's actions. The religious conflict—evil methods used to combat an evil—can be seen in a letter Brown received from a Quaker woman in Iowa: "You can never know how very many dear Friends love thee with all their hearts for thy brave efforts in behalf of the poor oppressed . . . [but] we who are [nonviolent] . . . believe it better to reform by moral and not by carnal methods."[12] Brown got this letter in jail while awaiting his execution. He wrote back to the woman, "You know that Christ once armed Peter. So also in my

Abraham Lincoln, who presided over the country during the Civil War, believed slavery was wrong, but considered Brown's raid a crime.

case I think he put a sword in my hand."[13] For Brown, resorting to bloodshed to end slavery was not a moral dilemma. His Calvinistic religion told him he was a soldier of the Lord and that, as a soldier, he must perform his duty.

One group of Americans—the African Americans—was unwavering in their devotion to John Brown. Slave or free, they considered Old Brown a God-sent figure, a mystic charged with the mission to liberate their race. African Americans worried little that Brown had blood on his hands from Kansas and from the Harpers Ferry raid. His friend and admirer Frederick Douglass said, "To the outward eye of men, John Brown was a criminal, but to their inward eye he was a just man and true. His deeds might be disowned, but the spirit which made those deeds possible was worthy of the highest honor."[14]

Brown's almost divine ties with African Americans were a theme touched upon by poets, artists, and songwriters. The crux of this theme lies in an incident that, as far as history knows, never occurred at all. Legend says that as Brown was taken to the gallows, a black woman, holding a baby in her arms, rushed up to him. Brown paused and warmly kissed the baby. Surely this incident is fiction. Brown was under intense, heavy guard, and the guards would never have permitted him the liberty of such a kiss. But artists have painted pictures of this mythical scene, and poets have been spinning the yarn for years. One such poet was John Greenleaf Whittier, who wrote:

John Brown of Osawatomie
They led him out to die,
When lo, a poor slave-mother
With her little child pressed nigh.
Then the bold, blue eyes grew tender,
And the old, hard face grew mild,
And he stopped between the jeering ranks,
And kissed the negro's child.[15]

A final reflection on John Brown lies in a question that has been discussed endlessly by historians: To what extent did John Brown's raid at Harpers Ferry bring about the Civil War? Certainly the raid shocked the country as did no other incident in the nineteenth century. Harpers Ferry united the Northern abolitionists and set them clamoring for war. The siege brought home to Southern society the nightmare prospect of slave uprisings led by Northern adventurers and financed by Northern money. Today, few people doubt that John Brown's raid at least hastened the start of the Civil War, which began eighteen months later. American writer Herman Melville, who wrote the classic novel *Moby Dick*, called Brown's raid "the meteor of the war."[16]

Historians generally point to two main sparks as igniting the great war: John Brown's raid on Harpers Ferry and the election of Abraham Lincoln. Though not an abolitionist, Lincoln was despised in the South. He was elected president in the fall of 1860. By the time he took the oath of office on March 4, 1861, seven Southern states had seceded (withdrawn) from

This 1863 painting is one of several drawings that contributed to the myth that John Brown kissed a slave woman's child on his way to the gallows. The kiss most likely never took place.

The Civil War was the bloodiest conflict in American history. More Americans were killed in the Civil War than were killed in World War I and World War II combined.

the Union. On April 12, 1861, Southern forces fired cannons at Fort Sumter, and the most destructive war in American history began.

The Civil War raged for four years, from 1861 to 1865. Some 620,000 Americans lost their lives in a string of bloody battles ranging from Texas to Pennsylvania. Slavery was the root cause of the war, and emancipation its result. Never during the Civil War was John Brown forgotten. Northern troops marched into battle singing a spirited song to the tune of what later became "Battle Hymn of the Republic":

John Brown carries a Bible and a gun in this 1937 mural called Tragic Prelude, *which was painted by John Stewart Curry on the walls of the state capitol in Topeka, Kansas.*

John Brown's body lies a-moldering in the grave,
John Brown's body lies a-moldering in the grave,
John Brown's body lies a-moldering in the grave
His soul's marching on!
Glory, Hally, Hallelujah!
Glory, Hally, Hallelujah!
Glory, Hally, Hallelujah!
His soul's marching on![17]

★ TIMELINE ★

1787—The Founding Fathers write the Constitution, which recognizes slavery.

1799—Slavery begins to fade in the Northern states, but it becomes more important in the South.

1800—John Brown is born on May 9, 1800, in Torrington, Connecticut, the third of six children, to Owen and Ruth Mills Brown.

1805—Owen Brown and his family move to Ohio, where John grows up.

1808—John Brown's mother dies.

1820—The Missouri Compromise allows Maine to enter the Union as a free state while Missouri enters as a slave state; John Brown marries Dianthe Lusk.

1832—Dianthe Brown dies; John Brown remarries to Mary Day within a year.

1837—Abolitionist Elijah Lovejoy is murdered by a mob in Illinois; At a service for Lovejoy, John Brown promises to devote his life to the emancipation of slaves.

1843—During a terrible epidemic of dysentery, four of Brown's children die within a few months of each other.

1849—Brown and his family move to North Elba, New York, where he continues to help slaves escape to freedom and where he plans to establish an African-American farming community.

1850—In the Compromise of 1850, Congress allows California to become a free state while the territories of Utah and New Mexico are left open to popular sovereignty regarding the slavery issue.

1854—Congress passes the Kansas-Nebraska Act, which creates two new territories and allows the voters of those territories to decide whether they want slavery.

1855—Brown and his family move to Kansas Territory to join the fight to make that territory a free state.

1856—On the night of May 24, Brown and a band of seven men drag five proslavery men out of their homes and hack them to death with swords in an event called the Pottawatomie Massacre.

1857—In the famous *Dred Scott* decision, the Supreme Court says that blacks—whether they are free or slaves—are not citizens of the United States and, therefore, are not protected by the Constitution.

1859—*October 16*: Brown and eighteen men (three others acted as rear guard) enter Harpers Ferry, Virginia, seize the federal arsenal there, and take hostages.

October 17: In the early morning hours, Hayward Shepherd, a free black townsman, is killed by one of Brown's soldiers; Militiamen from nearby towns arrive; Gun battles break out.

October 18: A unit of United States Marines commanded by Robert E. Lee arrives; The marines assault the engine house where Brown and his men are holding out; Brown is captured; Seventeen men, including ten raiders, are killed in the thirty-six-hour-long siege.

October 27: Brown's trial for treason and other charges begins.

October 31: Brown's trial concludes with a guilty verdict.

November 2: Brown is sentenced to death by hanging.

December 2: Brown is hanged in Charles Town, Virginia.

1860—Abraham Lincoln is elected president of the United States; Six weeks after his election, South Carolina becomes the first state to secede from the Union.

1861—*April 12*: Southern troops fire on Fort Sumter, plunging the United States into Civil War.

1865—*April 9*: Robert E. Lee surrenders his Southern forces to the North; Five days after the surrender Abraham Lincoln is shot and killed by John Wilkes Booth.

December 18: The Thirteenth Amendment to the Constitution, outlawing slavery in the United States, is ratified.

★ Chapter Notes ★

Chapter 1. Execution at Charles Town

1. Jules Abels, *Man on Fire* (New York: Macmillan, 1971), p. 368.

2. Stephen B. Oates, *To Purge This Land with Blood* (Amherst: University of Massachusetts Press, 1984), p. 351.

Chapter 2. A House Divided

1. "Lincoln's 'House Divided' Speech," in Jerome B. Agel, *Words That Make America Great* (New York: Random House, 1997), p. 192.

2. Geoffrey C. Ward, *The Civil War* (New York: Alfred A. Knopf, 1990), p. 9.

3. Eugene Genovese, *Roll, Jordan, Roll* (New York: Pantheon, 1974), p. 66.

4. Ward, p. 10.

5. Ibid., pp. 24–25.

6. Ralph Andrist, ed., "The Underground Railroad," *The American Heritage Making of the Nation* (New York: Bonanza Books, 1987), pp. 330–331.

7. Genovese, p. 72.

8. *The Annals of America* (Chicago and London: Encyclopedia Brittannica, Inc., 1976), vol. 4, p. 603.

9. "*Dred Scott* v. *Sanford*," *The Annals of America*, vol. 8, p. 442.

10. Andrew Carroll, ed., *Letters of a Nation* (New York: Kodansha International, 1997), p. 96.

11. Stephen B. Oates, *To Purge This Land with Blood* (Amherst: University of Massachusetts Press, 1984), p. 41.

12. Louis Ruchames, ed., *A John Brown Reader* (New York: Abelard-Schuman, 1959), p. 181.

Chapter 3. The Making of a Martyr

1. Stephen B. Oates, *To Purge This Land with Blood* (Amherst: University of Massachusetts Press, 1984), pp. 49–50.

2. "Sinners in the Hands of an Angry God," *The Annals of America* (Chicago and London: Encyclopedia Britannica, Inc., 1976), vol. 1, pp. 425–427.

3. Oates, p. 10.

4. Louis Ruchames, ed., *A John Brown Reader* (New York: Abelard-Schuman, 1959), p. 38.

5. Ibid., pp. 21–24.

6. Richard Warch and Jonathan Fanton, eds., *John Brown—Great Lives Observed* (Englewood Cliffs, N.J.: Prentice-Hall, 1973), p. 3.

7. Oates, p. 50.

8. Barrie Stavis, *John Brown: The Sword and the Word* (London: A. S. Barnes and Company, 1970), p. 22.

9. Ruchames, p. 184.

10. "A Letter Written by John Brown Jr.," quoted in Stavis, pp. 21–22.

Chapter 4. Soldier of God

1. Louis Ruchames, ed., *A John Brown Reader* (New York: Abelard-Schuman, 1959), p. 77.

2. "An Eyewitness to the Massacre," quoted in Ruchames, p. 200.

3. Barrie Stavis, *John Brown: The Sword and the Word* (London: A. S. Barnes and Company, 1970), p. 53.

4. Stephen B. Oates, *To Purge This Land with Blood* (Amherst: University of Massachusetts Press, 1984), p. 151.

5. Ibid., p. 240.

6. Ibid., pp. 282–283.

7. National Park Service, *John Brown's Raid* (Washington, D.C.: Department of the Interior, 1973), p. 18.

8. Oates, p. 289.

Chapter 5. John Brown's Raid

1. Jules Abels, *Man on Fire* (New York: Macmillan, 1971), p. 273.

2. National Park Service, *John Brown's Raid* (Washington, D.C.: Department of the Interior, 1973), p. 27.

3. Ibid., p. 34.

4. Edward Stone, ed., "News Reports," *Incident at Harpers Ferry* (Englewood Cliffs, N.J.: Prentice-Hall, Inc., 1956), p. 23.

5. Stephen B. Oates, *To Purge This Land with Blood* (Amherst: University of Massachusetts Press, 1984), p. 294.

6. National Park Service, p. 38.

7. Abels, p. 293.

8. Oates, p. 299.

9. Abels, p. 294.

10. Ibid., p. 295.

11. Ibid., pp. 294–295.

12. Richard Warch and Jonathan Fanton, eds., *John Brown—Great Lives Observed* (Englewood Cliffs, N.J.: Prentice-Hall, 1973), p. 65.

13. Abels, p. 297.

14. Oates, p. 302.

Chapter 6. Slavery on Trial

1. Louis Ruchames, ed., *A John Brown Reader* (New York: Abelard-Schuman, 1959), p. 315.

2. Ibid., pp. 118–123.

3. Jules Abels, *Man on Fire* (New York: Macmillan, 1971), p. 298.

4. Stephen B. Oates, *To Purge This Land with Blood* (Amherst: University of Massachusetts Press, 1984), p. 320.

5. Ibid.

6. Ibid., p. 318.

7. Ruchames, p. 267.

8. Abels, p. 320.

9. Ibid., pp. 320–321.

10. Richard Warch and Jonathan Fanton, eds., *John Brown—Great Lives Observed* (Englewood Cliffs, N.J.: Prentice-Hall, 1973), p. 82.

11. Ibid.

12. Barrie Stavis, ed., "A Statement by Virginia Governor Henry Wise," *John Brown: The Sword and the Word* (London: A. S. Barnes and Company, 1970), p. 148.

13. National Park Service, *John Brown's Raid* (Washington, D.C.: Department of the Interior, 1973), p. 53.

14. Ruchames, p. 126.

15. Abels, p. 331.

Chapter 7. The Death and Legacy of John Brown

1. Jules Abels, *Man on Fire* (New York: Macmillan, 1971), p. 334.

2. Louis Ruchames, ed., *A John Brown Reader* (New York: Abelard-Schuman, 1959), p. 143.

3. Stephen B. Oates, *To Purge This Land with Blood* (Amherst: University of Massachusetts Press, 1984), p. 338.

4. National Park Service, "A Proclamation from the Governor of Virginia," *John Brown's Raid* (Washington, D.C.: Department of the Interior, 1973), p. 56.

5. Oates, p. 350.

6. Ruchames, p. 158.

7. Abels, p. 367.

8. Ibid., p. 366.

9. National Park Service, p. 57.

10. Oates, p. 311.

11. Abels, p. 383.

12. Oates, p. 339.

13. Ibid.

14. Benjamin Quarles, ed., *Blacks on John Brown* (Urbana: University of Illinois Press, 1972), p. xiv.

15. Abels, p. 368.

16. Ruchames, p. 285.

17. Abels, pp. 390–391.

★ FURTHER READING ★

Books

Armstrong, Jennifer. *Steal Away*. New York: Orchard Books, 1992.

Barrett, Tracy. *Harpers Ferry: The Story of John Brown's Raid*. Brookfield, Conn.: Millbrook Press, 1993.

Hamilton, Virginia. *Many Thousands Gone: African Americans From Slavery to Freedom*. New York: Alfred A. Knopf, 1993.

Herda, D. J. *The Dred Scott Case: Slavery and Citizenship*. Springfield, N.J.: Enslow Publishers, Inc., 1994.

Katz, Tracy. *Breaking the Chains: African American Slave Resistance*. New York: Atheneum, 1990.

Kerby, Mona. *Frederick Douglass*. Danbury, Conn.: Franklin Watts, 1994.

Smith, Carter, ed. *Prelude to War: A Sourcebook on the Civil War*. Brookfield, Conn.: Millbrook Press, 1993.

Stein, R. Conrad. *The Underground Railroad*. Danbury, Conn.: Children's Press, 1997.

Internet Addresses

Letters Magazine. *John Brown's Last Letter.* May/June 1997. <http://www.signature.pair.com/letters/mayjune97/jbrown.html> (December 10, 1998).

The National Park Service. *Harpers Ferry National Historical Park*. August 5, 1998. <http://www.nps.gov/hafe/> (December 1, 1998).

John Brown Historical Association of Illinois. December 12, 1996. <http://www.cyberword.com/johnbrown> (January 27, 1999).

★ Index ★

TETON COUNTY LIBRARY
JACKSON, WYOMING

TETON COUNTY LIBRARY